View from a Birdcage

Flying Officer Jack Catford DFC

This story is dedicated to the crew of "W " Willie, my crew, both individually and collectively. Their companionship made light of the difficult times that we all endured.

First Published in Great Britain in 2005
by **TUCANN***books*
Text © Jack Catford
All rights reserved
Design © **TUCANN***design&print*

No part of this publication may be reproduced or transmitted in any way or by any means, including electronic storage and retrieval, without prior permission of the publisher

ISBN Nº 1 873257 49 X

Published by TUCANN*books*,
19 High Street, Heighington, Lincoln LN4 1RG
Tel & Fax: 01522 790009
www.tucann.co.uk

DEDICATION

The Unit	635 Squadron, 8 Group Pathfinder Force
The Station	Royal Air Force, Downham Market, Norfolk
The Aircraft	Lancaster 1 "W" Willie PB 914
The time	Mid January 1945
The target	Munich

The Aircrew

The Pilot	Squadron Leader Emile Mange - DFC and bar, RAF
The Navigator	Flt Lt Ernie Mawson - DFC, RNZAF
The Bomb Aimer & Nav II	Flt Lt Frank (Jacko) Jackson - DFC, RNZAF
The Wireless Operator	Flt Lt Cyril (Nobby) Clark - DFC, RAF
The Flight Engineer	Fg Officer Harry Wooding - DFC, RAF
The Mid-Upper Gunner	Flt Lt George (Red) Winch - DFC, RAF
The Rear Gunner	Fg Off Jack Catford - DFC, RAF

All ranks held at the time of the Munich operation.

CONTENTS

Chapter 1	Coming Events 5
Chapter 2	In at the Deep End 8
Chapter 3	Bridlington by the Sea 15
Chapter 4	Moving on - Bridgnorth 20
Chapter 5	Our First Flight - RAF Morpeth 27
Chapter 6	Returning to Yorkshire - RAF Driffield 37
Chapter 7	Crewing up at RAF Abingdon 40
Chapter 8	Heavy Conversion Unit - RAF Rufforth 47
Chapter 9	Combat 54
Chapter 10	Munich 57
Chapter 11	Press on Regardless 155
Chapter 12	War's End 169
	Appendix 188

CHAPTER 1
COMING EVENTS

In 1938 I had, in common with thousands of other men, volunteered for training as a fighter pilot in the Royal Air Force. After an anxious wait I received a reply from the Air Ministry. The letter was polite but firm - at that time there was no vacancy for me. I was acutely disappointed, though when I gave it some thought realized that although many thousands of such applications had been submitted, the Royal Air Force had at the most squadrons of Hurricanes and Spitfires totaling only some hundreds of aircraft. In addition, the Civil Air Guard had been in existence for several years, and had been able to turn out some hundreds of pilots trained to basic requirements.

In my disappointment, I turned to the newly formed Auxiliary Fire Service, joining this organization in September 1938. One year later I was a fully trained fireman, and for the first three years of the war I had all the excitement that I craved. Together with tens of thousands of other volunteers, we were thrown in at the deep end, in September 1940, when we were firefighting in the London Docks. Subsequently these duties took me all over London, including all the major city blitzes, as well as getting as far afield as Birmingham and Portsmouth when they were under heavy air attack.

For the first two or three years of the war I really felt that I was doing a worthwhile job. However by the end of 1942 the heavy Luftwaffe raids had all but ceased, and air activity in the main was reduced to spasmodic hit and run raids. As a consequence, I was desperately bored but salvation was on the way in the form of a letter from London Fire Brigade Headquarters. This stated that a release would be allowed from the Fire Service to any full time fireman, but only for aircrew duties in the Royal Air Force.

On my first leave day, with what my fellows termed "unseemly haste", I went along to the Joint Services Combined Recruiting Centre at Acton. I had already decided that I wanted to be: a rear gunner on bombers. If it had been feasible, my choice, like that of three years before, would have been for pilot duties. I knew, however, that a pilot's training took well in excess of a year, while the training of a gunner was only half that time. At the time, like many others, I thought that the war might well be over within a year, and I wanted to see some action; hence my choice. I went through my preliminary tests at Acton. These were relatively simple and I passed with no problems. At the end of these tests I was told that I should have to attend for a more lengthy session to be held over a period of three days during which time I was to be housed at a local hotel. The location of these further series of tests was to be at Euston House and I was told to expect a letter with details. Back I went to the Fire Station, delighted with the day's events.

Three days later the letter arrived instructing me to present myself at Royal Air Force, Euston House, taking with me my small kit since the tests would last at least three days. I duly reported and had a very busy time. There were many tests and examinations to be taken, mental, aptitude and physical. At last, after the passage of the three days, I was told that I had passed but that my final acceptance into the Royal Air Force was dependent upon my satisfying a Board as to my suitability.

The last afternoon came with my ordeal at hand. In company with a corporal, I was marched to the Board Room, and brought to attention at a table behind which was seated the Chairman of the Board, a Group Captain. The balance of the Board comprised a Wing Commander, and two Squadron Leaders together with four civilians. The Chairman addressed me, saying what was necessary, no doubt designed to put me at my ease though it didn't.

The questioning commenced and was very intense, everybody having a go at me. Eventually I was asked why I had chosen to be an air gunner, and I gave them my reasons which they appeared to consider satisfactory. Next the Chairman came up with what appeared to be a major hurdle. My tests had shown that I had an aptitude for wireless telegraphy, accordingly it was considered that my correct niche would be as a Wireless Operator / Air Gunner. What were my feelings? I replied that I still had a preference for straight air gunner. When asked my reasons I relied "for the same reason that I didn't want to train as a pilot, since I knew that a Wireless Operator/Air Gunner's training would last for close to a year'. The Board considered my reply, and then sent me out of the room whilst they deliberated amongst themselves. I sat outside, mentally chewing my knuckles for what seemed an unconscionable time, though probably only a few minutes. The wait came to an end and I was called, marched in and

Chapter 1 - Coming Events

stood at ease, and told that I was now enlisted in the Royal Air Force as air gunner (u/t). I was so overjoyed that I nearly saluted, remembering just in time that I was still a civilian, and not yet in uniform.

The corporal came in and I was about turned and marched out of the room and taken down to another room where I was duly sworn in, becoming one of His Majesty's newest potential air gunners. Later on that evening I was thinking about my ordeal before the Board and wondered if the reason why I was so readily accepted as a "straight" air gunner was because, at that time, the mortality rate for air gunners, particularly rear gunners, was very high indeed.

Following my enlistment I was told that I should be on deferred duty until the Royal Air Force were ready for me to commence my training. This could be a matter of several weeks, perhaps even a month or so. I was given lots of "bumpf", my Service Identity Card with my number 1893157, the latter imbedded in my mind for life. It was suggested that I spend part of the next six to eight weeks on studies, and to this end I was given a list of text books, some of which I purchased on my way back to the Fire Station. In addition it was suggested that it would be beneficial for me to join a local A.T.C. Squadron this for the time that I would have to wait until my call up was received. I duly joined such a Squadron at Wimbledon.

I now returned to my duties at the Fire Station which was situated at the All England Tennis Club in Wimbledon. Great were the celebrations upon my return. During the next few weeks I became involved in studies in navigation, aerodynamics, Air Force law and anything else that would be of use to me. During this period I put in a regular attendance at the local A.T.C. I was certainly the only person in the U.K. who during the balmy day's of May 1943 used to take my text books and climb up laboriously, right to the back of the Centre Court to occupy one of perhaps 10,000 seats. It was very quiet here, and conducive to studies, though I was still able to hear the Fire bells should there be a call out.

The days passed slowly with occasional call outs for "civil" fires, plus one or two sneak raids with the odd bomb dropped. To keep myself more fully occupied, I decided to go on a course for driving heavy goods vehicles. This training was done on an old red fire engine, quite a beast to learn on, though eventually I obtained my licence.

I continue waiting for the great day…

CHAPTER 2
IN AT THE DEEP END

Early in June 1943 I received the long awaited letter from the Air Ministry, requesting me to report to A.C.R.C. (Air Crew Reception Centre), at St. John's Wood, facing Regent's Park. I obtained my immediate release from the National Fire Service, my present employers, with whom I had served one year as a part time fireman, then full time since September 1939. Having attended a farewell celebration with all my fire service friends, I finally rounded up all of my accumulated gear, and left for home and my new life. I had been given 48 hours in which to clear up my domestic and private affairs. That night I called at the Air Training Corps Centre at Wimbledon which had looked after my pre-entry Royal Air Force training. The few weeks that I had been able to spend with them, two evenings per week, had been most useful and enjoyable. I had learned the Morse alphabet, and had progressed sufficiently to be able to send four words per minute, a very modest attainment, but of great help to me in my early Royal Air Force training. I had also picked up a smattering of navigation and Air Force law. All these subjects formed a fair proportion of my early training and stood me in good stead in the months to come.

The great day arrived, and with a modest suitcase, I set off for St. John's Wood and my new home. To allow for the great influx of potential aircrew, the Royal Air Force had taken over many blocks of flats in Prince Albert Road, facing Regent's Park. My "Station" was Stockleigh Hall, and eventually I arrived and reported to the Guard Room. From there I was escorted to the offices at Station Headquarters, and commenced my lengthy induction. Forms galore were completed and signed, and once more I presented myself at the Medical Centre for the gruelling aircrew medical. All went well, and in company with a dozen or so other recruits, we were marched back to the Squadron offices for allocation of quarters. Our mentor for the next four weeks was a corporal who wasted no time in making it quite clear that he was to be our Lord and Master during our stay. We were left in no doubt as to what would be our inevitable fate should we kick over the traces. Conversely, if we abided strictly

Chapter 2 - In at the Deep End

by the rules and regulations, we should be so happy that we would be heartbroken when we were posted.

We were escorted to our quarters; a three roomed flat on the third floor. It was very handsome accommodation but the furnishings were Spartan in the extreme. There were just the bare necessities, beds chairs wardrobes and dressing tables, and one communal rough deal wood table. The only floor coverings were strips of matting by the sides of the beds. We did find however that the Royal Air Force were generous to the extreme in the plentiful supply of cleaning materials. A cupboard in the hall was filled to overflowing with buckets, mops, scrubbing brushes, cloths, dusters, brooms and soap. We were told that the following morning, after parade and breakfast, we were to report back to our quarters to scrub and clean them throughout. Since it looked as though the outgoing airmen had only just completed the job it should prove to be relatively easy to do again. Our corporal informed us that unlike some of the blocks of flats, which were equipped with restaurants and kitchens, there were no such amenities at Stockleigh Hall. Therefore we should be feeding in the restaurant in the Zoological Gardens in Regent's Park. During the war the Zoo had been closed and the majority of large animals moved out into the countryside. As we quickly learned, this restaurant was an admirably run establishment with every facility that could be desired. During our stay we were extremely well fed, particularly after our very modest rations as civilians over the past years. As somebody said – "Like lambs before the slaughter"! The only real hardship in the messing arrangements was that after each training session we had a ten minute march to the restaurant, and ten minutes back again. This march, I would add, was at "cadet" rate, not a walk but rather a trot! The airmen who were lucky enough to be housed in flats which had messing facilities therefore had a lunch break at least twenty minutes longer than us since our marching time came out of the meal break.

At the commencement of our second day our corporal, true to his word, had us scrubbing and cleaning out our quarters. We were kept hard at it until NAAFI break. Being a hot sunny day, the break was more than welcome, even though inevitably over half of the short break was spent in an endless queue. After hurriedly eating the "wads" and swallowing the tea we lined up for the next ordeal. This involved us in a twenty minute walk to the other side of Regent's Park. We were to go to the main Royal Air Force Medical Centre, where we were to receive our 'jabs'.

This proved to be a real conveyor belt exercise. We were to have all

View from a Birdcage

the jabs at one go – tetanus, typhoid and smallpox vaccinations. Well over a hundred of us all lined up in a single file. Jackets were removed, and with both shirtsleeves rolled up we walked in one long line down a corridor with two medical orderlies part way down, one on either side of the corridor. Each was equipped with a large pad of cotton wool together with a bowl of antiseptic. As we passed them, they wiped both of our upper arms with the antiseptic soaked cotton wool pads. Continuing on, one came to three doctors, two on the left; we paused and each administered their vaccination, then it was the turn of the one on the right. The ordeal was over - talk about mass production! The most amusing part was picking out the "faint hearts". Strangely enough, it seemed that the bigger the airman, the more likely he was to faint. About 5% of our flight went a nasty colour, then keeled over onto the floor. A small batch of orderlies administered smelling salts, then picked the victims up and took them to a vestibule where they were left seated with their heads between their knees. They all seemed to recover quite quickly and with sheepish grins, being subject to ribald comment, they rejoined the ranks. Soon after this we marched back to the Zoo for a meal. The evening was spent doing sundry chores and fatigues. At this stage of the training we were not allowed out of the station. When our work and duties were over we studied our textbooks, played cards or wrote letters, with a bit of reading thrown in. We also had a NAAFI designated room where light refreshments were available. By lights out we had retired deadbeat, with the knowledge that the next day we were to go to Lords Cricket Ground, the local R.A.F. Clothing Stores, where we would finally be kitted out.

After breakfast the next day we were lined up in Squadron order, ready to march off to the clothing parade. There was much jubilation in the ranks – at last we would feel that we were really airmen. Personally I did have a few minor reservations about being dressed in uniform, mostly concerning creature comforts. So far into our initial training the weather had been fine and very warm. Once we were attired in our uniforms we were going to be very hot. Our present attire, mainly sports jackets and flannels with open neck shirts, were much better suited to the mid summer temperatures, and would soon have to be put away for the duration. The things that I dreaded most were the boots to be worn all the time we were cadets. Horrifying stories abounded about the miseries to be endured with our new footwear. Indeed, the morning sick parades were largely composed of members of the previous intake just one week ahead of us, having treatment for foot trouble. The final blow was that as soon as we

Chapter 2 - In at the Deep End

were in uniform we should be eligible for sundry guard duties.

Off we marched at 8.30 a.m. sharp, to the cricket ground which was half a mile along Prince Albert Road. We were ushered through the main gates, thence to the huge clothing store situated beneath the Grand Stand. Having been formed into single file, we marched along the counters, stopping briefly at each to collect an item of gear. The first item issued was the kit bag into which went an amazing collection of articles. With the exception of cap, shirt and boot issue, we were not asked our sizes or measurements. The airmen behind the various counters cast an experienced eye over us, went to a rack and returned with a complete uniform that was dumped in front of us. Surprisingly, when we returned to our billets and tried them on, there were very few items needing to be exchanged. In the majority of cases, once short leave started, airmen's wives, mothers and sisters effected the minor alterations required.

We were returned in time for NAAFI break and afterwards we were sent back to the billets to sort out gear and dress ourselves as airmen, or else! The number one requirement was to get a shine on the tunic buttons and cap badges. They were horribly tarnished, not having been touched since leaving the clothing factory. Our kit included a button stick, and most of us had already bought polish and a duster from the NAAFI ready for the great day. Work went on apace in our flat. Eventually, all the buttons and badges were gleaming. I suppose that the proudest possession at that time was the little white "flash" which fitted into the front of the caps. This denoted that the wearer was an aircrew cadet. Next, the horrifying moment arrived when for the first time we donned our boots. They were not too uncomfortable whilst we were standing around, but we dreaded the thought of marching in the days to come. Once more we got "fell in", an oft repeated and monotonous occurrence. This was to be our lot for months to come.

The march or trot commenced, through the Park and into the Zoo, eventually arriving at the restaurant. We were sticky and sweaty in our unaccustomed dress. At this stage our feet were not too bad, just hot and tight. Regrettably, this was to alter within the next few days. We sat down to the usual ample meal – this happened to be one that I long remembered. One of the vegetables served was asparagus – a particular weakness of mine. I commenced the mouth watering repast, and half way through the meal, noticed that the airmen on either side of me did not touch their asparagus. Upon enquiring why, they each presented me with their unwanted portions. My plate was piled up, inches high until finally it was cleared. What a feast! Whom one sat with at meal times was a matter of chance, and never again was I able to sit between them though this was not for want of trying.

When we returned to Stockleigh Hall, the corporal stood us at ease whilst he went into the Squadron office. After a short time he was back with an ominous typed list in his hand. He commenced to read out the guard and fire picket duties for the next seven days – I had drawn two of each. From this moment on we commenced our routine lectures and drills and had barely a moment to call our own. Lectures were on many subjects with particular reference to Air Force Law. We also studied basic navigation, Morse code and Aldis lamp signaling, as well as a minute study of "K.R's" (King's Regulations). Much attention was also given to physical fitness, and P.T.; running and swimming were daily occurrences.

The week passed slowly by and each day our feet became more sore and painful. The one thing that boosted our morale was that when this weekend arrived, we should have reached the half way mark in our stay at A.C.R.C. and we would all become eligible for a week end pass. Although we had only been in the Service for two weeks, it already seemed a lifetime. Finally the weekend arrived, and on parade our passes were handed out. I had a hurried dinner and then went to the Guard Room and booked out. As soon as I was out of the Station I walked across the road to a bus stop. Under normal circumstances I would have enjoyed the pleasant walk across the park, and would have caught a train from Baker Street station. Now all that I desired was to get the load off my tired and aching feet. Just walking at a normal pace and sitting down on a soft bus seat was marvellous! An hour later, with a brief stop off at the local shops, I arrived home. My first action was to put on a kettle of water, and when it was hot pour it into a bowl and immerse my aching feet. The joy and comfort was indescribable. I turned on the radio and stayed put for over an hour, occasionally adding more hot water to the bowl. Later I called at the local chemist shop and purchased various potions that I rubbed into my feet. With what bliss I retired! The weekend passed by on fleeting wings; I had telephoned two Fire Service friends and we had a very happy reunion at the "local". Arriving home at a late hour I slept like a log. All too soon I was back at Stockleigh Hall, and on duty.

Following my return, I was reminded that I had an early 4 a.m. gate Guard Duty the next morning. Two of my buddies in the billet had returned off pass with feet so bad that they had to report on sick parade the next morning. They were not made particularly welcome since allowing one's feet to get into such a bad condition was second only to that most serious of crimes – self inflicted injury! As it happened, their feet were so raw that they were excused boots and allowed to wear black shoes whilst the healing process took place. At the end of our stay they were walking normally and back to wearing the regulation boots. The pampering that I had given my feet over the weekend had paid rich dividends, and following my return I had no further foot trouble, becoming quite at ease in boots.

Our studies, drills and P.T. continued without too many problems, and it was only in our final week that I fell foul of Military Law, and suffered my first dose of "jankers". (military punishment) It happened that I was on guard at the Main Gate, complete with Lee Enfield Rifle. The mail had been taken round and one of my roommates brought a letter down and slipped it into my hand. In view of the importance of the occasion I was not as sensible as I should have been. I glanced around and saw no one, the street out side was deserted, and so I carefully placed my rifle against a stone gatepost, opened my letter and commenced to read it. A few seconds passed then I heard a menacing bellow of "Airman"! I very hurriedly put the letter in my pocket, picked up my rifle and resumed guard duties. There was still no one in sight, but all too soon, from behind me, I heard the heavy clumping of Service feet, and the choleric face of the Flight Sergeant (Discipline) peered at me from close quarters, saying "When your guard duty has finished, report to me at the Discipline Office". Two hours later I received from him what is know as a right royal dressing down. I felt so small that I was afraid that I should fall down a crack in the floor: every evening for the rest of the week I had no free time. Even the evening trip to the NAAFI was barred to me, though my roommates kept me supplied with sustenance. I reported after duty each day, and spent the evenings washing and scrubbing anything that needed or didn't need, cleaning. I was surprised at the number of latrines that there were in Stockleigh Hall. – I got to know them all very well. The only lucky thing for me was that my dereliction of duty had taken place after my weekend pass. This I would have certainly forfeited had I been caught out the week before. This banning of leave had been suffered by at least a dozen chaps in our intake, and very sad faces they had been when we left the Station on pass. Upon reflection, I suppose that the old saying "it's an ill wind" etc. held true on this occasion because the twelve "Janker wallahs" were just sufficient to do guard duties over the weekend.

View from a Birdcage

The alternative, depending upon the luck of the draw, was that we should have to break into our weekend leave by reporting back for an odd 2 or 4 hour stint of guard and fire picket duty.

At last our time at A.C.R.C. drew to a close. On Friday morning our postings were announced. I found that I was posted, with all my roommates, to No.14 I.T.W. (Initial Training Wing), Bridlington, Yorks. It was just the right weather to enjoy the seaside. We were to leave at 7.30 a.m. on Saturday morning. We were out of bed by 6 a.m. and as P.T. was cancelled, we went straight to breakfast, afterwards returning to our billets. These had been scrubbed out the night before though we had no doubt that the incoming flight would have to set-to and give it another scrub on Monday. We packed all of our gear into the kit bags, put on our great coats (the temperature was in the high seventies), donned our webbing, packs and gas mask cases, with steel helmets strapped thereto, and got fell in on the parade ground. At 7.30a.m. sharp the lorries arrived and on we clambered. Fifteen minutes later we arrived at King's Cross Station, got off the lorries and marched into the station and on to a platform where a York train was waiting. A short time later we were on our way to the next stage of our training.

CHAPTER 3
BRIDLINGTON BY THE SEA

Three hours later we arrived at York, where we were to change onto a local to Bridlington. With some effort we managed to get all our gear safely off the train, and on orders from a corporal, we lined up at the back of the platform. After a short time we were told that there would be a wait of 45 minutes before the train was due to arrive, and we could go into the refreshment rooms for a snack. Most of us had already finished the packed lunches that had been supplied at breakfast time, so this was welcome news indeed since we were again hungry and very thirsty. Fortunately we happened to be adjacent to the door of the refreshment bar; we dashed in and were at the head of a long queue that immediately formed. Five minutes later we were sitting out-side on our kit bags eating sandwiches and sticky buns, and drinking welcome cups of tea. After a stand-easy of thirty minutes we were lined up once more, ready for the arrival of the train. It soon arrived and we all piled in and were on the last lap of our journey.

None of us knew how long the journey would be. Based on distance it shouldn't have been more than an hour at most, but with the uncertain travelling times of these days, the trip took just over two hours. We played cards and I looked for the first time at the magnificent Yorkshire scenery through the Dales and Moors. We arrived in mid afternoon, tired but content.

Once more we were lined up in the station yard where a roll call was taken. Half a dozen corporals were listening to an officer who was reading details from a list. Eventually, each corporal was given a short typewritten roster after which they came over and separated us into Flights. Each Flight contained approximately 40 airmen, each with a corporal in charge. All my buddies were with me in B flight. The corporal introduced himself and gave the usual lecture on discipline. He seemed quite a decent chap and we were hopeful of a happy stay.

On arrival we had no clue where we would be staying, though we imagined that it would be one of the R.A.F.'s requisitioned hotels. In fact, Station Headquarters, together with sundry offices, were in such a hotel,

View from a Birdcage

but we were all to be billeted in requisitioned guest houses. We were soon on the march into town. When we arrived in a road close to the cliff top we were halted, and twenty of the airmen were detached from our flight and marched into the empty looking guest house. The corporal stood us at ease and followed the airmen into the house while we waited outside for five minutes. He then returned and marched us off to another house in the same road. We went into our new billet. Take an empty house, put into it the minimum furnishings together with the inevitable strips of matting, and a cupboard full of cleaning materials, and you have our home for the next four weeks!

We sorted out our belongings, and with half an hour to spare, lay on our beds and relaxed. After the brief rest I got up and explored the rest of the house. On the ground and first floor that we occupied were four bedrooms, kitchen, loo and bathroom. The top floor contained two more rooms which were locked and not in use. I assumed that they were used by the Royal Air Force for storage space, or maybe the owners of the house had stored their belongings therein. The kitchen looked promising, until I discovered that the gas was cut off. We used it as a common room for reading and writing – though alas, no tea and hot snacks before going to bed.

The time for assembly had arrived. We were five to a room, and I banged on the doors to arouse the occupants. We got fell in outside the premises and marched up the road, joining the corporal and the rest of the Flight. After a few minutes walk we arrived at S.H.Q. outside of which, the other Flights were assembling. After a brief delay, we marched into the Dining Hall for our first meal. The food was up to the usual high standards that we had enjoyed at A.C.R.C. and not long afterwards, replete and tired, we assembled outside and marched back to the billets. The corporal told us we were free for the evening and warned us to "watch it" while we were in town – no doubt meaning the drinking! The following morning, after we had breakfast, we would return to the billet and scrub it from top to bottom.

Our evening of freedom was much enjoyed by all. Excluding the midterm weekend pass when we were in London, this was the first time that we had been let loose on our own since joining the service, and we tried very hard not to let it go to our heads. The town was reasonably full of summer visitors, despite the war, and we were happy to find that most of the beaches were open unlike the mined beaches on the south coast. We wandered around, content with our unusual freedom, visiting pubs and amusement arcades. It was nice to discover that the locals made us very welcome. Half of the present population seemed to comprise of R.A.F. bods, mostly aircrew cadets, and I suppose that the dwindling trade from the civilians was largely offset by members of the R.A.F. which must have been a useful boost to the local tradespeople. I was tempted to try the dance at the Pavilion, but by late evening I was very tired so finished my perambulations with a short walk along the beach, then back to bed for a night's kip.

At 7.30 a.m. the following morning we marched to breakfast, returning by 8.30 when we got stuck in to the scrub up. Our corporal visited us in mid-morning, casting his basilisk gaze over the floors etc. There were a few criticisms, but not too much. The NAAFI wagon called and stopped at the front of the house and a brief break was allowed for tea and wads. By midday we had finished and assembled at S.H.Q. for dinner. Afterwards, the entire new intake was marched to the pier where we gathered in the theatre for an address by the C.O. We were given an outline of the training that we were to undergo, largely an extension of that which we had already embarked upon, and again an emphasis was placed on P.T. The two additions to our curriculum were Morse signalling with the Aldis lamp, and shooting which pleased us immensely particularly in view of our aircrew categories.

We had our first firearms tuition the following day. Fortunately the fine weather continued unabated and we were marched along the beach to the gun butts. To my great delight, I learned that our initial instructions were to be on 12 bore sporting guns which were considered to be the most suitable guns to get one's eye in, since the targets at which we would shoot would all be moving and coming at different angles. On the beach there were three skeet throwers, each set to fire in a different direction. After a brief lecture on the safety rules and the range regulations, the shooting commenced with an instructor teaching us the basics prior to our firing. I can honestly say that at no time before or after this occasion did I enjoy shooting so much. During my entire service I had the opportunity of firing practically every type of firearm which could be used by one man - revolvers, automatics, Sten guns, Bren guns, Lanchesters, Lee Enfield and Garand rifles, all of varying calibers plus Brownings and even hand grenades – including, eventually, German stick grenades! My first favourite remained the 12 bore sporting gun.

The shooting continued, and although my previous shooting experience had been confined to .22 rifles and an assortment of air guns and pistols,

View from a Birdcage

I soon got the hang of the 12 bore. It took only a couple of trial shoots to confirm what our instructor had stressed - the need to hold the butt of the gun firmly into the shoulder. Any slackness by anyone using the gun in this respect resulted in a very pronounced kick which in turn could badly bruise the shoulder. That night many an airman revealed purple bruises when he undressed – so always follow instructions to the letter! One of the most satisfying things which I had ever experienced was my first bull with the 12 bore when the clay disc at which we were shooting shattered into hundreds of pieces. During these practices, which were to continue for the four weeks of our stay, we always had an admiring audience in the public. They watched us in their hundreds from the safety of the cliff top, and some could be seen making bets on those airmen who appeared to be crack shots.

The days passed quickly and most enjoyably. We had by now become proficient with our Morse, both sending and receiving. The arrangements for signalling were quite good. Half of the Flight stood on the beach with pads and pencils reading messages sent to them on the Aldis lamp by the other half of the Flight who were on the end of the pier. At half time in the exercise we changed round which gave everybody a chance to send and receive.

During our stay at Bridlington we had plenty of swimming to which had been added a new dimension – dinghy drill. Those of us who could already swim, probably about 80% of the Flight, did our swimming in the sea. The non-swimmers, under tuition, used the swimming pool. All aircrew had to be able to swim by the time that their training was

Our wing- ITW, Bridlington

18

completed, and I never heard of any non-swimmer who failed to qualify by the time that the training at I.T.W. was at an end.

We had two companies from E.N.S.A. visit us, performing their shows in the theatre on the pier. These shows were most welcome and enjoyable, and both featured well known actors and actresses. We were also regular visitors to the cinemas during the evenings. Altogether we really enjoyed our stay in Yorkshire, not least because of the friendliness of the natives who so obviously went out of their way to make us welcome. On several occasions I was invited home by local families. Towards the end of our stay we had our first flight photograph taken and were very pleased and proud of the result. Only a year later it was with a feeling of great sadness that I knew that over half of those happy faces had been killed or were missing.

CHAPTER 4
MOVING ON - BRIDGNORTH

Our last day at Bridlington arrived, and we gathered at the Squadron Offices to find out where we had been posted. When at last I reached the head of the queue in front of the notice board, I found that I was to go to R.A.F. Bridgnorth, in Shropshire. This was an E.A.G.S. (Elementary Air Gunnery School). Again the bulk of my chums were on the same posting, which pleased us all as we gathered outside, excitedly discussing the latest move.

The next morning we were on our way. It proved to be a long long journey, since for some reason we went via Liverpool. No doubt this was due to wartime expediency, since it was not usual to have to travel right across England from east to west before turning south! After a most tiring day we arrived at Bridgnorth at dusk. Fortunately we had again been supplied with a packed lunch when we left Bridlington. It was just as well we were wise and didn't eat it too soon, because on this occasion there was no waiting when we changed trains at Liverpool. Our day had been exceptionally long and we were now ravenous and deadbeat. A fleet of lorries was waiting for us and we were soon on our way to our new Station. In the gloom we couldn't see much of the town, but what we saw, we liked. We drove slowly to R.A.F. Bridgnorth, which was about three miles from the town, sitting astride a hilltop on the other side of the valley. By now it was pitch dark and we had arrived at the camp. We were dropped off at various Nissen huts, our billets, and unloaded our gear. Afterwards we climbed back onto the waiting lorries and were driven to the Mess Hall for a meal. We ate ravenously, after which we were marched back to our billets where we collapsed onto our beds prior to retiring.

We soon learned that the town was divided into two parts, High Town and Low Town. High Town was on top of an escarpment, about 200ft high, and one was able to look over a cliff edge to Low Town below. By road, traffic went down a pretty steep hill. Pedestrians could ride down on a cliff lift similar to those at several seaside towns. There were also a number of steep paths and roads for those preferring to walk. When first visiting the town by daylight we were really impressed. It was most attractive, and quite old. At the foot of the cliff the River Severn wound its way around Low Town. During our stay we did hear that Bridgnorth had more pubs per inhabitant than any other town in Britain. How true this was I never found out. Maybe it was an exercise in advertising! Anyway, there were certainly an awful lot, and during our stay we sampled most of them.

After breakfast on our first morning at the new camp we gathered for our introductory lecture. The curriculum was similar to that of our previous postings but more advanced. There were one or two additions, including a series of lectures on evasion in enemy territory. These were of great interest to us, and one of our instructors was an air gunner who had already baled out over the other side and after some quite amazing adventures in the hands of the "Underground", with whom he fought for some months, had returned home via Spain. This he did in about five months, a reasonably short time in view of the conditions and distances involved.

As part of our introduction we were marched around the camp, learning where everything was. I knew that I going to enjoy the lovely countryside visible all around. We had a brief stop in a hangar for NAAFI break, then on with the march, finishing up at the billets for a thirty minute break before going on to the Mess for dinner. It was no surprise to be told that during the afternoon we should be engaged in scrubbing out the billet. We had seen on our walk where the camp NAAFI was situated, and this was much enjoyed during our stay. It was possible to get a hot snack during the evening as well as tea, coffee and beer. There were billiard tables and dartboards, quite a club atmosphere, though far more crowded than any civilian club would normally be. During our training thus far we had always been in civilian accommodation and so had not had the benefit of a NAAFI club in which to relax.

Next morning our lectures commenced, and we quickly learned of the major problem with which we should be faced whilst at this Station. The lecture rooms were nearly all in wooden huts, and in the high temperatures that we were enduring they became overpoweringly hot. For the first time in our training we had to fight against falling asleep during the lectures, particularly since the penalties for such occurrences could be severe. We did have one lecturer who seemed to realize how we suffered – even he became sleepy eyed at times though to our regret

View from a Birdcage

he never dropped off. When he caught any of us asleep it was usually followed by a severe dressing down. With other lecturers it was jankers galore. For reasons unknown we were kept on camp for the first 72 hours after our arrival, but eventually the day arrived when we were allowed out after duty. There were buses into town, but they were rather irregular so our party decided to walk the three miles which were largely downhill. Our first evening was very enjoyable, and we were able to explore both High and Low Town in the daylight. We liked what we saw, and in fact Bridgnorth proved to be the nicest town throughout our training. We tried many pubs which in the main were filled with members of the Royal Air Force. Our first evening ended with a smashing fish and chip supper, after which we had to run for the last bus back to camp. We just managed to catch it. Fortunately the conductor was a good sort and allowed us all on to his already grossly overcrowded vehicle. It was a miracle that the driver was able to get the bus up the very steep hill out of town.

The next morning we had an enjoyable stint on the range firing .303 Lee Enfields, Sten guns, and for the first time, .38 Smith and Wesson revolvers. Overall I was lucky with my score that morning. Unbeknown to our instructors we had hurriedly arranged a sweepstake of one shilling per head – winner take all. On this occasion I won it, though the prize melted away like snow in hot sun when we went to the NAAFI that evening. Lectures were now in full swing, and that afternoon I had the first of many frights in trying to combat an overwhelming desire to sleep. Despite the best of intentions, I nodded off several times. Luckily I was awakened each time by a dig in the ribs from the student sitting next to me. Later during the same lecture, I was able to return the same compliment, which was just as well because the lecturer in this class was a hard liner and jankers would have been his answer.

We quickly learned of the desirability of getting into class early so that a seat at the back of the classroom was obtainable. Falling asleep in the front rows was to be avoided at all costs, since a dozing airman was clearly visible to the lecturer. In the back rows one stood a better chance of being unnoticed. Throughout our stay at Bridgnorth, the hot summer weather continued with only one short break at the end, consequently each day brought a fight to avoid dropping off to sleep. This problem was aggravated by the non stop P.T. and games in which we indulged.

During the middle of our second week in camp we were told that we could apply for a 48 hour pass. The news was received with delight. That night the main subjects for discussion in the NAAFI were our plans for

Chapter 4 - Moving on - Bridgnorth

the weekend. The bulk of the airmen plunged for a visit home as many lived not far away. The train service to London was not too frequent, and involved at least one change, perhaps more, so I decided to spend my weekend at Wolverhampton which was only 45 minutes away by bus. I had a longing to see the bright lights, even though they were now pretty dim, and civilization sounded very attractive. The most important thing was that the town contained two very large Service clubs, the "Y.M." and the "Sally Army". It was possible to book bed and breakfast in either for two shillings per night.

The next two days seemed to creep by, and on Friday after duty I joined the queue at S.H.Q for my pass. Together with a friend who was coming with me, we walked the half mile from the camp gates to the main Wolverhampton road where we waited for the bus. After a few minutes of waiting, a motorist pulled up and offered a lift which was gratefully accepted. In just 30 minutes we were dropped off in the centre of Wolverhampton. Our first evening was terrific - first a visit to a pub, followed by the cinema, and finally eating at a fish and chip restaurant. At 11.30 pm we set off for the Y.M. When we arrived, what a shock! They were full to overflowing with no chance of any accommodation. Even the lounges and passages were packed with sleeping servicemen. Off we set hopefully for the Sally Army, but on arrival it was the same story; no accommodation available. Far too late we realized that we should have booked a bed as soon as we had arrived in Wolverhampton, and then gone off to enjoy ourselves. During my Service career thereafter, I never again made the same mistake.

On the advice of the reception girl at the Sally Army, we were directed to a certain church being informed that the Vicar left it open at night for waifs such as us. He was an avowed Christian with Christian ideals. With some difficulty in the blackout we found the church and went inside. There was no one at the door and no lights inside. It was pitch dark, but as soon as we got inside the cacophony of snores, in all keys, confirmed the use to which the church was being put. Dimly we could see that all the sleeping bodies were on pews, and we squeezed past them until we found a space big enough for the two of us. We searched around and found a couple of hassocks for use as pillows, and settled down for what proved to be the most uncomfortable night that we had ever spent, in or out of the Services. I managed to get a few cat naps throughout the night, but the narrowness and hardness of the benches plus the snoring precluded any further rest.

At last the grey early light slowly turned to sunshine, and as early as possible we set off for the Y.M. for a clean up and breakfast. Fortunately, both were available, and after an enjoyable repast we went to Reception and were able to book beds for that night. Our day in town passed very pleasantly and we met up with many buddies from our camp, one of whom we learned had spent the night in the same church as us. When evening came we decided that we had had enough beer, so we went back to the club and had a meal, this being followed by a restful evening playing snooker and darts followed by a sing song that threatened to raise the roof. By ten o'clock we were dead tired and went to our cubicles where we made up for the lack of sleep on the previous night. On Sunday we continued with our tour of the town and had a pub lunch. By the time that evening arrived we were too tired to stay any longer, so made for the bus station catching the 7.30 pm bus back to Bridgnorth and arriving at camp soon after 8.30 pm. We made a quick call at the NAAFI for a cup of tea and a bun, and were in bed by 10.00 pm happy and tired and, we hoped, ready for the next week's labours.

After breakfast the following morning I learned that I had been drawn a guard duty that night. Not a very auspicious start to the week, though in fact there were not too many of these duties, and I only had to do this one during the whole of my stay on camp. We had another visit to the range and this time my score was well down, so the beer wasn't on me that night. During the afternoon the inevitable fight against sleep was fought in the hot wooden huts. Six of us were caught out, including me. Fortunately, the friendly lecturer was in charge, so we endured the acceptable wigging. Thereafter the door was left open, bringing in a sluggish movement of air that eased the problem.

My guard duty that night was 12 pm to 2 am, so prior to this I was able to get into town for the odd drink and the inevitable fish and chips. By now we had discovered the pub of our choice, and spent most of the evening there, playing darts and quaffing the local brew – very nice it was. Halfway through the evening there was a squealing of brakes, and a jeep pulled up outside. Three rugged S.P.s appeared in the bar and turned the place over. We all had to produce our 1250s (Service identity cards) and were given a clean bill of health. We never knew who or what the S.P.s were looking for.

I arrived back at camp at 10.00 pm, in time to take an hour's nap on the bed before reporting to the guardhouse for my duties. Upon arrival I signed on, collected my rifle and mounted guard on the gate. It was a

Chapter 4 - Moving on - Bridgnorth

very pleasant evening, moonless but lots of stars, and I found the two hour stint not unpleasant. During my time on the gate, the jeep and S.P.s returned together with two very drunk airmen, one singing loudly and the other vomiting over the back of the jeep! They were locked up in the guardhouse and once again peace descended. The area seemed to abound in owls that kept up a non-stop hooting, with occasional flurries in woods and hedges as they pounced on mice and other luckless rodents. At 2.00 am sharp my relief arrived and took over my duty. I returned to the guardroom, surrendered my rifle and booked off watch. As I left I could hear the airman in the cells still vomiting! I enjoyed my first cigarette during my walk back to the billet where I thankfully dropped off into a good night's sleep.

The next day was not one of my best. During the afternoon between lectures we were being marched to the next lecture room. This time I was busy explaining to a friend, what a "zombie" was! We were passing a hangar at the time, and craftily hidden round a corner of it was the Station Warrant Officer (Discipline), busily watching us as we marched. He stepped out into view, halted the Flight and signalled me to come out to the front. Many of us had been talking – and I suppose that mine was the loudest voice! He enquired why I was talking and what I was talking about. With hindsight, I realise that it would have been wiser if I had said that I was discussing a problem that had arisen during the last lecture. When I unwisely explained that I was telling a friend what a "zombie" was, the Warrant Officers face turned a funny colour! (He must have thought that I was having him on) "Report to my office A.D." he said.

When the afternoon lectures were duly over, I reported to his office and was given my second dose of jankers since joining the service – "Report for duty at the cook house at 1800 hours" he said. Upon arrival, the Sergeant in charge put me on the usual nightmare job of peeling potatoes. There was a huge mountain of them, I swear not less than 10cwt., so I commenced the soul-destroying job. At 2200 hours I was released from bondage. I had by then peeled about 3 cwt and my fingers were raw. At least during my stay they had fed me well. Many were the bacon sandwiches that I had consumed, washed down with countless cups of tea. I am happy to say that this was the last time in my service career that I did jankers.

The last week of our stay at Bridgnorth was coming to an end, and all was worry and excitement because, for the first time since training had begun, our results thus far were to be assessed. From Tuesday onwards, we should be taking examinations and tests, and on the Friday afternoon, we were assembled to learn the results of our labours. When at last I heard them, my cup of happiness was full! I had achieved 6th place out of our class of 40, and was overjoyed with this result. Later that day, our posting notices appeared on the board at S.H.Q. I found that I was posted with all my friends, to No.4 A.G.S. (Air Gunnery School), situated at R.A.F. Morpeth, just north of Newcastle.

CHAPTER 5
OUR FIRST FLIGHT - RAF MORPETH

This was our most exciting move so far, for it was at this station that for the first time we were going to fly! For weeks we had been talking about it, and various rumours had reached our ears. Someone whose cousin was ahead of us on the same training course had already passed through No.4 A.G.S. and had now gone on to O.T.U. (Operational Training Unit). While he had been at R.A.F. Morpeth he had been flying in Blackburn Bothas, not the most successful of wartime aircraft. They were of all metal construction and word had it, that because of design, if you crashed in the sea, which on occasions happened, there was little chance of getting out alive!

Apparently because of weight and design, they tended to go straight down to the bottom of the sea unlike many training aircraft which were buoyant enough to float for a while, thus enabling the crew to get into the dinghy, or at least swim away. Over the grapevine we heard, much to our relief, that all Bothas had been withdrawn from training command, and in the majority of cases had been replaced by Ansons, these aircraft having been equipped with mid-upper gun turrets. When we eventually arrived at Morpeth we learned that this rumour had been true which made us very happy. The old "Annie" was a very nice aircraft in which to fly, and was very popular with pilots and aircrew and with us in due course.

Another pleasure to look forward to was at the end of our course at No.4 A.G.S. we should be taking our exams, and if all went well we should be awarded our "tapes" (Sergeants' Chevrons). We were now well into autumn and our last days at Bridgnorth saw a change in the weather, two days of grey skies and drizzle together with a much lower temperature than we had experienced since joining the Royal Air Force. For the first time our waterproofs were unpacked. These also doubled up as ground sheets. Marching around camp was not nearly so pleasant, though sleeping during the few remaining lectures tailed right off. Fortunately, by Friday, the weather began to clear up.

During our last night at Bridgnorth we had a regular booze up in town and bade farewell to the many friends that we had made. By 7.30 am the following morning we were getting aboard the train for York where we changed onto a Newcastle train. It was a long journey, but as usual we had been given a packed lunch. Remembering the last journey, we did not forget to fill our water bottles on this occasion. Drinking beer on the journey was strictly forbidden, but some airmen bought beer and used it to fill up their water bottles with it. As a result, there were some very flat drinks on offer! After a long dreary journey we arrived at York. The Newcastle train was waiting for us, so once more there was no opportunity to obtain refreshments. The train was very full and most of us had to sit on our kit bags in the corridor. I managed, with a few others and with permission, to get into the guards van. At least we had space there and were able to spread out in relative comfort.

We arrived in Newcastle after a reasonably quick journey and had to change onto a local train. The 15 minute wait enabled us to tend to the wants of nature; nothing having been available in the guards van. Afterwards we managed to obtain cakes and a cup of tea from a trolley. Finally we were on our last hop, and after a short journey pulled in at Morpeth. The S.W.O. was waiting for us, and as soon as we were off the train he lined us up on the platform and gave us what he probably thought was a welcoming lecture. Without a doubt, he was to prove to be the most unpopular man in authority that we had so far encountered. What a nasty piece of work he was! During our stay we avoided him like the plague and happily for us, and probably for him, we gave him very little reason to complain.

In the station yard the lorries were waiting, and 15 minutes later we arrived at No.4 A.G.S. R.A.F. Morpeth. The station was fairly high up on the moors and looked attractive. Certainly the temperature was decidedly lower than it had been at Bridgnorth, and we had visions of what it would be like here in the winter. We piled into the Mess Hall for a hot meal which went down very well since our packed luncheons had been consumed many hours before. Eventually we were taken to our billets, Nissen huts again, where we quickly settled in. We passed the evening in the very nice NAAFI and retired early.

In the morning the N.C.O. in charge of us – a sergeant this time – introduced himself. We were not in the least surprised to be told that immediately after breakfast we were to return to the billets and scrub them out. The food in the Mess was particularly good and we hoped that it would continue to the same high standards that we had so far enjoyed.

Chapter 5 - Our First Flight - RAF Morpeth

In fact, it did. After breakfast we marched back to the huts and busied ourselves with our domestic morning.

By the time that NAAFI arrived we had finished all our chores. The Sergeant came round and carried out his inspection. By now our cleaning was up to professional standards, and all was well. After the break we marched to the Crew Room on the airfield where we were to be addressed by the C.O. It proved to be the most welcome induction so far. Our first week in camp would mostly be spent in the lecture rooms. Nearly all new subjects - airmanship, theory of air firing, Browning .303 machine guns and lots more dinghy drill. Providing that there was not too severe weather, dinghy drill was to be carried out in the sea, fully dressed! We were also to have more skeet shooting with the 12 bore guns. The physical side had not been forgotten. Daily P.T. would continue and in addition we would be playing rugby and indulge in an 8 mile cross country run. At the end of the first week we were to have our first air experience flight. We were told the sad fact that on each new intake of potential air gunners there were a few who on their first flight were airsick. If they suffered this indignity they were given at least two more flights because the excitement of the first flight might have contributed to the nausea. If after further flights they continued to suffer from airsickness, they were taken off aircrew duties. Although this may have seemed unfair, this action was based on sound common sense since any member of a bomber crew who was likely to be sick on operations was a menace, both to his crew and to himself. On our course there was only one airman who was taken off flying duties for this reason. He had been so ill during his flying that he welcomed being taken off aircrew duties and being given a ground job. It was sad that this could happen, because nobody knew in advance how they would stand up to flying. Conversely, once this flying test had been passed, you were in, and there was no turning back!

As soon as we had arrived at Morpeth it had been confirmed that the Squadron had recently been re-equipped with Ansons and we also discovered that all our pilots were Free Poles. We soon found them to be excellent and gifted pilots with a dash of daring which made flying with them a lot of fun. After dinner on that first day we were all marched up to the hangers and given a guided tour of the Anson. The only difference between this aircraft and those that we had seen flying elsewhere was that all of our aircraft had been equipped with a mid upper gun turret. We were told that the "mark" that we should be flying did not have hydraulically retractable undercarriage. Because of this, the required drill, when airborne, was as follows. Each aircraft carried three gunners under training. One got into the turret, one sat on the main fuselage floor, and the third sat in the co-pilot's seat. It was necessary for the undercarriage to be retracted and let down manually, and the gunner sitting next to the pilot was the undercarriage operator. On orders from the pilot, he retracted the undercarriage by winding a wheel, which was equipped with a small handle. This was situated between the two pilot seats. It took an awful lot of turns to complete the operation! Completion of the act was shown when two little green bobbles showed at the top of two tubes adjacent to the winding handle. The same drill, but turning the handle in the reverse direction, lowered the undercarriage - naturally a much easier job.

The pilots encouraged the students to ask any questions, and we wasted no time in putting these to them. We were thoroughly enjoying our practical training and now it was time to be introduced to the Browning .303 machine gun which was the normal armament for all British bombers. Later in the week we should be firing them live on the station ranges where they had two Frazer Nash rear turrets erected on concrete bases. After half an hour's talk and demonstrations, we sat two to a table on which a Browning M.G. was placed. We commenced, under expert tuition, to strip the guns down to their component parts after which we had to reassemble them. We were informed that at the end of the course we would have become sufficiently proficient to strip them down and rebuild them wearing a blindfold! Excellent training if we were to have trouble with the guns whilst flying on operations at night. There seemed to be so much to be learned about the guns that we did wonder whether we would ever get it buttoned up. Of course we did, despite these forebodings.

Our last session of the day was P.T., and we were told that on the next day this period would be used for a game of rugby, a game I had never played before. Each course also had to run the eight mile cross country race. This would take place next week, and we were all entered! The day ended and after tea we returned to the billets. We were allowed out every night after duty, and the local town of Morpeth was within easy reach without the need for transport. It was a quiet little town with a few nice pubs, and an occasional dance. For those who wanted to jazz it up, Newcastle was within easy reach by train or bus. It offered the usual glamour of the big cities. All the normal service clubs were to be found there, and available for overnight stays. We were told, that subject to the usual exigencies of the service, 48 hour passes were issued each weekend.

On the following morning we had our first lectures in the use of pyrotechnics. This lecture included a thorough briefing in the various types of cartridges which were used in the Brownings – ball, armour pierce, incendiary and tracer, Verey pistols and their cartridges, signal flares, rockets, photo flood shells and an outline of the various types of bombs which we should be carrying on operations, During the afternoon we went up to the airfield and practiced firing the Verey pistol, signal flares and rockets. A large school of rooks in the nearby poplar trees scarcely moved. Obviously they were used to the weekly firework display.

At day's end we decided to stay on Camp to have a session in the NAAFI, then early to bed in preparation for tomorrows P.T. The previous night we had gone down to Morpeth and had thoroughly explored the town. It had been quiet but we all liked the little place and were made welcome in the pubs. That weekend I had decided to stay in Newcastle. Next morning we attended lectures on airmanship and the theory of sighting when airborne. Both lectures were very interesting, particularly on sighting, and it was at that lecture that we learned that on our first air firing exercise we would be using camera guns. The results would be assessed on the ground the same day. These early exercises on the camera guns were particularly useful to our instructors, enabling them to correct pupils before any bad habits became entrenched. We should also be going to the ranges where the four gun turrets were set up. This would be the first opportunity that we should have had to fire the guns that we should be using when we were operational.

Friday arrived, at long last! This was the morning that we were to have our first air experience flight, the culmination of all our ambitions so far. Thereafter we would be flying every day. As the pilots said "We're going to fly your pants off". We were marched up to the airfield and into the clothing store where we were fitted out with helmet, having attached the intercom and oxygen mask. Next came the Sidcot flying suit, flying boots, parachute and harness, gauntlets and finally the Mae West. This gear would be retained by us while we were stationed at Morpeth, and lockers were supplied in which to store it all. After the issue of clothing we returned to camp for dinner. Flying began in the early afternoon, and I noticed that most of us ate sparingly - just in case!

We returned to the airfield at 2 pm and were sorted out into crews of three and then assigned to pilots and aircraft. At this stage we were issued with what was to become our most treasured possession, our personal flying logbook. Every flight that we ever did was entered therein, and to this day it has pride of place on my bookshelf.

My pilot was Sergeant Danieluk who collected us and walked us over to a long line of Ansons. Skipper as he was known was very friendly and outgoing and we all got on very well together. Climbing aboard our aircraft, the engines were started and after a brief run up we throttled back to tick over while we waited for our "green " (a flash on an Aldis light) from the caravan at the beginning of the runway. This would denote that we could safely commence the take off. In due course we taxied out to runway 27. I had drawn Pilot's assistant and was sitting by his side, so had a very good view of the proceedings, as well as being responsible for winding up the undercart. The Sergeant put on the brakes and revved the engine hard. Quickly he released the brakes, and we slowly rolled forward rapidly gaining speed. After bouncing a couple of times we were airborne.

It was without a doubt the most exciting experience of my life, and I gloried in every moment. The pilot signalled me to commence winding up the undercart and I bent down and began this laborious job. It seemed to go on for ever and a day, but eventually the two green bobbles appeared. The pilot gave me the thumbs up, whereupon I settled back to enjoy myself. On this occasion there was no gunnery exercise as it was purely an air experience flight. The sky was part cloud covered and the camp that we laboriously marched around each day looked diminutive. I was fascinated watching all the instruments, and saw that we were moving at 130 m.p.h. at a height of 7,000ft when we levelled out. The Sergeant headed for the nearest patch of cumulus cloud and our trip and enjoyment had really commenced. We did a steep dive into the clouds and as soon as we were in the cotton wool, we climbed steeply out of the cloud then back into the valleys between the clouds, then back again into the sun on top. It was a quite marvellous experience. Superimposed on the white edge of the cloud along which we were flying, we were being pursued by the shadow of our aircraft, sometimes the moisture in the air making a circular rainbow around this shadow. It was quite fascinating. We continued to do steep dives and climbs, then had a couple of practice stalls when it felt as if we were going to fall out of the sky. Finally we approached the flat top of a cloud and practiced landing on it. Altogether my cup of happiness was full, having had the thrill of my life. Afterwards when I had given it some thought, I believe that the fairly violent manoeuvres which we had undergone were deliberate, being designed to test our standards for flying and our digestive juices! The three of us felt fine and equally thrilled. I had a strong feeling that our Polish pilot also enjoyed himself. It seemed

Chapter 5 - Our First Flight - RAF Morpeth

that the Polish pilots generally had a touch of daredevil in their flying, something which in the Battle of Britain many German pilots had learned to their cost.

The following day we were on the range to test fire the Brownings - this was another exciting experience. When I first fired the guns I was lucky enough to see a most unusual phenomena. Each of the four guns was firing at a rate of 1200 rounds per minute. The sun was low on the horizon behind me as I fired. Suddenly I became aware that I could see the four streams of bullets leaving the guns in a straight line and burying themselves in the sand banks at the other end of the range. These bullets looked like an endless stream of gold fish. The Sergeant in charge told me that this was because of the low angle of the sun directly behind me, and that it was rare for the bullets to be seen leaving the guns.

That night I had drawn my first guard duty, and it was the dreaded 2 till 4 am stint! Together with another airman, my duty was to patrol a small blister hangar on the edge of the airfield. At 1.30 am we were awakened by an S.P. and quietly dressed ourselves. The night was clear and frosty, almost the first that we had so far experienced. With greatcoats on we reported to the Guard Room, signed on and were given our rifles and dispatched to the airfield.

We duly relieved the guard and commenced a brisk walk around the structure that we were to guard. This walk was as much to keep warm as to keep out interlopers! After 10 minutes or so my curiosity got the better of me and I went inside the hangar. Its contents proved to be huge stacks of Hessian sacks, contents unknown. I prodded them and they were agreeably soft. It was then that the great idea occurred to me. The patrol area was small enough to be effectively guarded by one man, therefore why not split our watch into two? One could be on guard whilst the other slept or rested on those nice soft sacks. We were both in agreement and after tossing a coin, I retired to the comparative warmth of the hangar to be awakened in one hours time, or immediately if there be any sign of activity, when I would take over my guard.

I clambered onto the pile of soft sacks, took off my great coat and covered myself with it, and was quickly asleep. After an hour, which went by in a flash, my buddy awakened me and took over my nest. The moon had arisen and the first hard frost of the autumn sparkled under its dim radiance. I was glad to keep briskly on the march, around and around the hangar. Five minutes before the end of our watch I awoke my companion, and we were both outside when our relief arrived a few minutes later.

View from a Birdcage

Back at the billet we were able to snatch a couple of hours kip before getting up for ablutions and breakfast. During the morning lectures I gradually became aware that I was itching all over. This became steadily worse, and by dinner time it was driving me round the bend. It was then that I learned that my companion on the night watch was also suffering from the same symptoms. To some extent this relieved me, since I had feared that I might have contracted chickenpox or some similar disease. After dinner we quickly returned to the billet for a hurried shower which to some extent relieved the intolerable irritation. It continued for several days before dying away. By then it had become obvious to us, that the itching was in some way tied up with our guard duty. Upon close examination of our uniforms we had found that they were impregnated with very fine silvery fibres. We made discreet enquiries among the stores personnel which resulted in the solution to the miseries from which we had suffered. The sacks in the hangar contained fibre glass wool used for insulating the exhausts and heating systems of aircraft. These fibres were extremely fine and worked their way through the sacks and our uniforms, finishing up imbedded in the pores of our skin! Thus had my idea of skiving on guard duty come home to roost!

The previous weekend I had obtained my pass and enjoyed a weekend in Newcastle. We arrived there early on Friday evening, and profiting by our experience in Wolverhampton, went directly to the Sally Army and booked beds for two nights. Over the weekend we visited the cinema twice, also went to the local dance hall which was very entertaining. We sampled the pubs, walked along the Tyne, visited the shipyards and went to Jesmond Dene, eventually arriving back at camp on Sunday night tired but happy. The remaining weeks at Morpeth were spent equally in the lecture rooms and in flying. Our flying hours were mounting up. By now we were engaged in air firing exercises all the time. On the first three flights we used cine guns. The film was processed the same day and the post mortems held in the last training session. Many were the laughs and blushes during these early days, but this particular aspect of training paid off and marked improvements in sighting were made within a very short time. Thereafter we continued with pukka firing at towed targets, and occasionally on targets mounted on rafts floating in the sea nearby.

The day came when the cross country race took place. Over 200 of us were lined up, and off we set. After a punishing first three miles I got my second wind and actually began to enjoy myself. The race was over the moors - not the easiest place to run. To my surprise and delight I

Chapter 5 - Our First Flight - RAF Morpeth

finished 21st out of the 200 runners. Since I had never previously run more than about three miles, I was very pleased with myself! There was no doubt that the strenuous life and regular P.T. had improved our physique tremendously. Never before had I felt so fit, and this being so, my first game of rugby came as an anti climax. For the benefit of novices, which included me, the P.T. instructor had explained the rules of the game. The match commenced and for the first five minutes I did a hell of a lot of running around, but rarely saw the ball. Suddenly, from out of the sun, it fell at my feet. I grasped it and ran wildly towards the goal, then the end of the world seemed to have arrived and I found that I was at the bottom of a pile of bodies. When finally I was able to get up, I was completely winded and suffering from chest pains. I was taken to the station sick quarters where I was examined and pronounced alive. Just for good luck I was strapped up with two inch tapes, and told that I was fit for duty. After 48 hours the pain had gone. Back I went to the sick quarters where they promptly ripped off the tape, giving me much more pain than that I had suffered on the rugby field!

The next day we were flying, firing at drogues towed by Harvard trainers and a few clapped out Hurricanes. The attacks by the fighters were very exciting to us novices. Some were from the beam, which involved the attacking aircraft commencing a curving attack aiming in a spot in the sky well ahead of its target, so that by the time that the attacker was in a position to fire its victim had moved into its sight and range. This was known as "a curve of pursuit attack". Other attacks were made from near enough dead astern, the fighter either climbing up from below or diving down from above. This type of attack was known as either a "QXO" or "QXU" (quarter cross over or quarter cross under). During exercises each gunner fired his own tray of ammunition and each gunner's bullets were stained with a different coloured dye, thus when the drogues were released from the fighter aircraft and dropped to the ground, they were picked up and taken to the gunnery section where the hits by the three gunners were easily separated and properly apportioned. The exercises on the floating targets at sea made a change. These were particularly enjoyable because they had to be made at low level and it was quite good fun flying over the sea at about 100 feet. The sensation of speed was wonderful.

The last week at Morpeth arrived and we took all the exams and tests, passing out with flying colours. My markings were reasonably high and I felt very content with my lot. Friday was the day to look forward to, and although our training was far from finished it was up to us, the culmination

View from a Birdcage

Our Wing- Air Gunnery School, Morpeth. August 1943

of all our ambitions. On this day we would be awarded our Sergeant's "tapes" (chevrons), and even more important, our Air Gunner's Brevet. There was a "bull" parade, after which we marched up individually, to be presented with our tapes and brevet. That night, off came our cadet flashes, and on were sewn our tapes and brevets, after which we pointedly called each other "Sergeant".

CHAPTER 6
RETURNING TO YORKSHIRE - RAF DRIFFIELD

The next day I was posted, together with a few of my friends, to R.A.F. Driffield battle school. This was back in Yorkshire. We went by lorry and the journey only took about two hours. This was only a seven day course but was very strenuous and all action from the word go. We had practice parachute jumps from a tower, many hours of work in the gym which included learning how to fall on the ground correctly, unarmed combat, boxing and cross country running; in fact everything except swimming. This was just as well because winter had arrived early and the water was freezing. We had quite a lot of frost and some light snow. More lectures were given on the art of evading, and at a later date some of the less fortunate members of the course undoubtedly profited from what they had learned after they had bailed out over on the other side.

The climax of the week's course was the evasion exercise. We would be driven in a covered lorry many miles from the airfield and dropped off in the pitch dark with absolutely no idea where we were. The idea was that we had to find our way back to Driffield and cross over the perimeter of the airfield without being caught. To make matters more difficult, the police, Home Guard and R.A.F. S.P.s were to be out in force with the object of capturing us before we were safely home. The day of the exercise arrived, and at 10.00 pm we mounted the lorries and set off into the darkness, having no idea where we were going or in what direction. The lorry drivers took a circuitous route to further confound us. We were in uniform but all that we were allowed to take with us, having been searched beforehand, was a packet of biscuits and a shilling!

We traveled for about an hour and a half - the time was guesswork since we had no watches - and eventually the lorry slowed down and made the first stop, dropping us off in pairs. We subsequently learned that releases were made at ten minute intervals. Our turn came, with only two others left. Off we got watching the dim tail light of the lorry vanish down the road. The sky was cloud covered and there was a little light snow. We had no greatcoats, but luckily ground sheets were permitted. We had no logical reason but despite this felt that we had been dropped south of Driffield, distance unknown. Allowing for the circuitous route that the lorry had travelled, we felt that we were probably 15/20 miles away from camp.

Having come to a joint agreement we set off on what we believed to be due north. As no compasses had been allowed, a good sense of direction was vital. We walked for about two hours, partly along roads and partly countryside and moorland. In those days all signposts had been removed as well as plaques containing place names. We passed the odd house and occasional village, although if we saw them in time we avoided them for fear of lurking police or soldiery. Surprisingly, we were not cold and after walking for what we guessed to be about three hours, we heard the hissing of steam from a stationary train. We cautiously approached an embankment and peered down. In the cutting below was a long goods train with open trucks waiting for a signal to change from red. The very old tank engine was pointing in the direction in which we wished to go – that is where we thought north to be. After a brief discussion we decided that the chance was too good to miss, so we quickly clambered down the embankment and climbed onto an empty truck. Five minutes later we were on our way.

The train trundled along at a very modest speed, no more than 20 miles per hour, and we stayed with it for about 30 minutes. By this time we were getting cold. Eventually we went through a small station that we recognized as being only a few miles from Driffield. Our hunch had paid off; we had chosen the right direction when we had been cast adrift. A few minutes later the train slowed down, finally stopping at a red signal. We wasted no time jumping off and taking to our heels. The sky had cleared it was very cold and dawn was near with the first lightening of the sky to be seen. During our train ride we had become frozen and welcomed the opportunity of getting warm again. We avoided the road surfaces and trotted along the grass verge making not a sound.

We neared the airfield, and for the first time saw the Police and Home Guards prowling around. We dropped into the frost covered bracken and, after deliberating, decided that it would be better to split up, each trying to make his own way back to camp. We separated and half an hour later I was within sight of the airfield perimeter. By now the sun was up and it was a beautiful frosty morning. I scuttled across the road and was just the width of a field away from the perimeter when I saw two S.P.s coming my way. They hadn't seen me so I dropped into a ditch and waited for them to pass. After a few minutes all was quiet and I carefully lifted my face. I saw no one but had a strange feeling that I was being watched. I peered around slowly, and saw in a low hedge on the other side of the ditch a large dog fox! We looked at each other for several seconds then he dived deep into the hedge and scuttled away. Five minutes later I crawled under the wire and had made it! I walked round the perimeter track, waving to the odd "enemy" S.P. and went straight to the cookhouse for a cup of tea and a warm. Shortly afterwards I sat down to an enormous breakfast and was pleased to be joined by my chum, also successful in getting back un-captured. After this we went back to the billet where we spent the day in bed. That evening in the Sergeants Mess we were chatting to our instructor. We learned that nearly half of us had returned safely, a lot more than usual since the average number of successful evaders was usually about 20%.

CHAPTER 7
CREWING UP AT RAF ABINGDON

Our final day at Battle School arrived and at assembly I was notified of my posting to no. 10 O.T.U. (Operational Training Unit) at R.A.F. Abingdon near Oxford. The most exciting thing about this course was that it was here that we should be crewed up. On Saturday we left by train for Oxford from where we would be picked up by lorry and taken to Abingdon. The usual pattern followed except that as Sergeants we were not involved in scrubbing! For the first time we now had no need for the NAAFI, other than the van when we were out on the airfield. We had automatically become members of the Sergeants Mess. The quarters were exceedingly comfortable after our somewhat Spartan surroundings of earlier months. Despite being mess members however, we still had to occupy Nissen huts for sleeping purposes. There wasn't nearly enough room in the Sergeants Mess for that purpose, bearing in mind that 90% of the aircrew on courses were Sergeants. The bedrooms in the mess were occupied by Staff Sergeants and it would have needed a mess the size of the Albert Hall to accommodate all of us.

During the first week we were to crew up, which was pretty exciting. Our new skipper (pilot) was Flight Sergeant Doug Houghes, an Australian, and our navigator team were two New Zealanders, Ernie Mawson, Navigator and Frank Jackson, Bomb Aimer and Nav.II. The nav. team had recently been commissioned and were Pilot Officers. I was particularly pleased to meet Red Winch, he being the second air gunner and my other half. He also had been commissioned recently, and had been in the Royal Air Force before war had been declared. Our new Flight Engineer was Sergeant Harry Wooding, and our Wireless Operator Sergeant Hank Turner whom regrettably we were to lose from the crew before we commenced operations.

It was most enjoyable moving around the Station as a complete crew. Our flying together was to commence in a few days time. We attended many lectures together, but separated on occasions when we had to attend lectures relating to our own particular trades. Although discipline was still

Chapter 7 - Crewing up at RAF Abingdon

firm, as Sergeants we now had a lot more freedom and privileges. It was probable that we outnumbered the airmen on the station 2 to 1 - all Chiefs and no Indians! A brief settling down period passed and the time arrived for flying to commence as a complete crew. Once more we were flying aircraft which we had never flown before. These were Whitley bombers, and with reservations we found them very good aircraft in which to fly. They were all metal, low winged monoplanes with twin Rolls Royce engines. They were at least twice the size of the old Anson, though with a lot less room in which to move. A large part of the fuselage was taken up by the bomb bays and we were now a full crew of seven. Happily the undercarriage was hydraulically operated – no more winding it up! The aircraft was equipped with two gun turrets, mid upper and rear.

At about this time the decision was to be made as to who was to be the rear gunner and who the mid-upper. In the event of there being no amicable decision reached between the two gunners (which was rare), then the skipper made a choice. If after this there was still disagreement, the Squadron C.O. made the decision, and that was final. For no reason that I know of, I had always seen myself as a rear gunner. When I first discussed this with my other half, we found to our delight that Red favoured being the mid-upper. What a happy coincidence - no problems involved. In another way the choice worked out well. There was more headroom in the mid-upper and Red was the taller. I was 5ft 8$^1/_2$ inches tall. This was just about the maximum comfortable height for the more cramped rear turret, although I did know of rear gunners of around 6ft – most uncomfortable.

Our flying training now commenced in earnest, and it was non-stop. For the first week, Duggie our pilot flew as a pupil. Although he had already earned his wings, his previous flying had been on different aircraft, and he now had to pass out on the Whitley with a pilot qualified on that type to check him out. This took just one week, and he then did a couple of solo take offs and landings following which he was then certified as competent on this type of aircraft. Thereafter there was no co-pilot, and we were all happy to have Doug at the helm.

From now on not a 24-hour period passed without us being airborne at least once each day, followed by a night trip. These flights were based on the need to give each member of the crew air experience in his particular category. As a result we had Navexes (Navigational Training Exercises) galore, and for the gunners air combat exercises. These air combats involved the use of cine camera guns, as well as firing live ammunition at drogues which were towed by aircraft. These were usually Martinet machines - quite fast single engine monoplanes.

One of these Martinet aircraft humbled my pride! Towards the end of our training at R.A.F. Abingdon we had been on an exercise with one of these planes towing the drogue. They were twin seat aircraft though the pilot usually flew alone. On this particular day, when we had finished our flying in the morning, I decided that it must be an intcresting experience to be a passenger in the attacking aircraft. I went along to the fighter flight and had a word with the C.O., asking if I might fly as a passenger in a Martinet engaged on an air firing exercise. He was quite agreeable and sent me off with one of the staff pilots to go on a trip. I climbed into the rear cockpit and settled down, ready to enjoy a new experience. We took off to rendezvous with a Whitley over Swindon. It was a most invigorating trip, the aircraft feeling so light and fast after the lumbering Whitleys.

Eventually we sighted our target and gave the pilot a flash on the Aldis. A curve of pursuit attack commenced with the drogue trailing some hundreds of feet behind us. I was surprised at the violence of movement in this much lighter aircraft, far more than in the old Whitley even when it was under attack. We made a dozen attacks before completing the exercise, by which, and for the first time, I felt violently airsick. I took a lot of deep breaths, thanking my lucky stars that we were now flying straight and level! By the time that we landed my stomach had settled down and I was very thankful indeed that I hadn't committed the ultimate sin of vomiting all over the cockpit floor. Apart from the disgrace it would have been my job, rightly so, to clear up the mess. I imagine that my colour must still have been a bit "off", because as we walked to the Flights the pilot asked me if I was all right? I lied in my teeth and said "Fine". I never again flew in a very light aircraft until the war was over, nor did I tell my crew of my narrow escape from disgracing myself. After that trip I was never to feel airsick again, even though on operations we sometimes flew in extremely bumpy conditions, particularly in cumulus nimbus cloud when we experienced shattering dives and climbs at least as severe as that which I had just experienced.

For the first time since leaving A.C.R.C. months before, I took the opportunity of going home on a weekend pass. So much time had gone by since my last visit that I felt like a stranger in my own home. The empty flat was tidy, as I left it, but full of dust. I set to and performed my own domestic evening, then went over to see my mother where I spent the night. My next port of call was to visit the Fire Station and see all my old friends. I received a great welcome, and in deference to my stripes, a number of salutes! As this brief sojourn drew to an end I was surprised that I was looking forward to my return and being once again with the crew who by now were my closest friends.

We commenced our third week of flying, enjoying every minute of it, even though we did seem to be a bit short on sleep. Following my return, our first flight was a night Navex. Take off wasn't until 2 am and we had a longish trip, up to Scotland and return. It was a clear night, no wind and reasonably mild. There was a moon for the first two hours of the journey. We loaded up taking with us a big box of rations containing sandwiches, barley sugar, raisins and chocolate together with several flasks of coffee. In addition we had a supply of caffeine tablets in case anyone felt sleepy. The trip went well and the old Whitley droned on effortlessly. Twice on the journey north we gave searchlight batteries an exercise (by prior arrangement). On one occasion we were "coned" and now knew what to expect when it was for real. Although the Whitley was a fairly large aircraft, it wasn't particularly roomy inside with all sorts of equipment and obstructions along the fuselage. To clamber from my turret it would have helped if one had been a contortionist.

It was not a particularly fast aircraft, being happiest at its cruising speed of about 140 m.p.h., but it was very stable and not too noisy. One peculiarity was its nose down flying attitude and one could never mistake a Whitley flying when viewed from the ground. When flying level the rear gunner was about 6ft higher than the pilot. Its landing characteristics were also unusual due, I believe, to the exceptionally wide wings. When approaching the runway for landing it floated down and because of this, rarely made a bumpy landing. All the aircrews liked flying in these aircraft, although we should have had grave reservations if we were flying them on operations since they were lacking both in power and speed for sustained combat against enemy fighters. Even so, they had been used in operations earlier in the war and had had some small successes in raids on the enemy.

Our trip was coming to an end and daylight was close. There was thin cloud below and we couldn't see the ground. In our pre-flight briefing we had been told that one of the station Martinets would be rendezvousing with us 50 miles from base to carry out a fighter attack sortie. This meeting was overdue and we eventually received a message by radio from Abingdon informing us that because of inclement weather, the sortie

View from a Birdcage

was off. When we were within about 15 minutes flying time from base, they again contacted us on radio and told us that because of fog we were to divert to a satellite station, R.A.F. Stanton Harcourt, and land there. Stanton was about 15 miles from Abingdon where conditions were clear enough for landing. We touched down at 7.30 am without any incident and after debriefing the M.T. sent a lorry round to pick us up. We were taken to Oxford railway station where we embarked on a train to Abingdon. We piled into the back of the lorry, in full flying kit, with parachutes slung over our shoulders. When we reached Oxford station we created a sensation when we appeared, dressed as we were, on the platform! It was crowded with commuters and we assumed by their expressions that they thought that we had successfully baled out of our aircraft. We got back in time for a late breakfast and bed. During the morning the fog gradually cleared and a spare crew were sent over by Anson to bring our aircraft back.

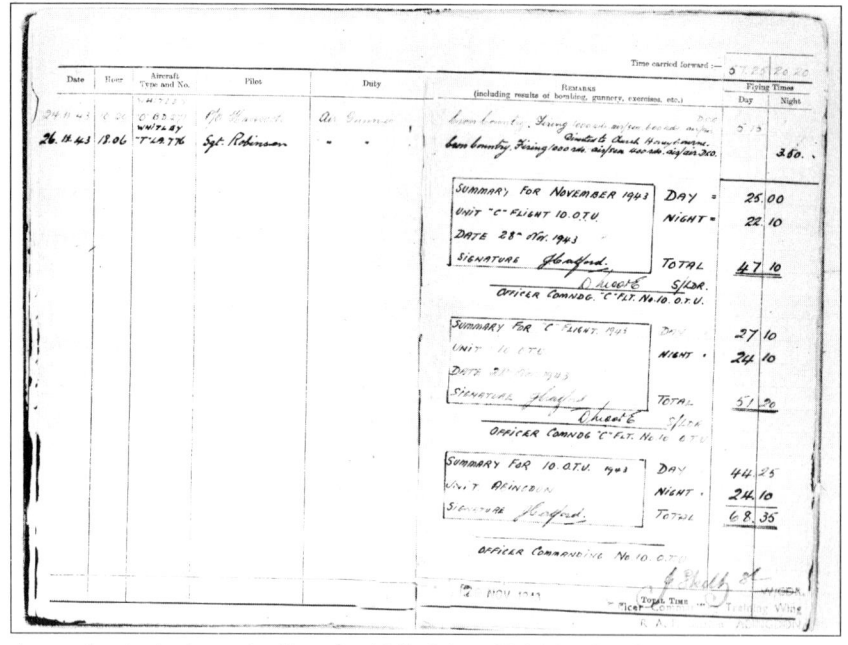

A page of my log book covering November 1943 whilst at 10 O.T.U, Abingdon.

Our time at Abingdon was drawing to a close, and the highlight of all our past training was approaching. This was a flight over enemy territory. The purpose was to give the crews their first experience of flying over enemy territory under operational conditions. Bombs were not carried;

Chapter 7 - Crewing up at RAF Abingdon

instead we took bundles containing many thousands of propaganda leaflets that were to be dropped over enemy held territory in western France. This particular type of raid had been in force for some considerable time and hopefully had boosted the morale of the underground, as well as the ordinary citizens. The target, so the whispers said, was to be in the Cherbourg area, which in the past had been a popular target, and the trip was not too long lasting about $3^{1}/_{2}$hrs. in all. Past experience had shown that there were occasional German night fighter attacks on the Whitleys and one or two had been lost. Generally however the trip was considered to be a bit of a doddle.

Wednesday arrived, and the six crews taking part in the exercise arrived at the Briefing Room. These aircraft were split up into two operations. For three of them the target was Cherbourg (which included us). The other three were to go a bit further west, in the region of Nantes. Our take off time was 11pm and the Nantes raid an hour later. After briefing we all gathered in the Crew Room and dressed in our flying clothing, Mae Wests and parachutes. In retrospect, I realised that we were all very excited and pent up – our non-stop chattering and joking was symptomatic of such an occasion.

We went out to the aircraft 30 minutes before take off time. Everything was checked and double checked. The engines were started and after a brief run up were pronounced O.K. They were then shut down and we had to endure a 15 minute wait before take off time was due. At 10.55 we started up the engines once more, and after a few minutes taxied out to the runway and took off. We climbed slowly towards the operational height of 14,000 feet, putting on oxygen masks at 10,000 feet. The darkness below was complete; only once did we see any lights. These were from a Royal Air Force airfield to the south west of Abingdon which was engaged in night flying. By the time we crossed the English coast we were above oxygen height, and shortly afterwards levelled out at 14,000 feet. Talking was kept to a minimum and all was quiet. Gradually we approached the French coast. Our course was west of the Channel Islands where the Germans were known to be operating fighter airfields. We were also routed west of the Cherbourg peninsular on which there were extensive concentrations of heavy flak guns. As soon as we crossed the coast of France we were routed 15 miles inland, then had to turn to port, running up over the outskirts of Cherbourg. It was hoped that this route would keep the local defences uncertain of our eventual target. We were close to the French coast when suddenly to the east of us the German flak batteries opened up. To our inexperienced eyes, it was a frightening display of pyrotechnics and I was glad that it was at least ten miles away from us. I was sitting on the edge of my seat, searching the skies intently. Some minutes later we experienced our first fighter attack. I had vaguely noticed, in a patch of the sky to our starboard, that a small segment of the stars were missing! I suddenly realised the significance, switched on the intercom and said to Duggie, "Fighter attack developing on the starboard quarter – dive starboard…GO" The old Whitley dipped down into a steep dive and corkscrewed over to starboard. At the same time a stream of tracers came from what I could now see was a single engine fighter. Red and myself quickly opened fire, and the attack was broken off. We had lost 2,000 feet and slowly we started our slow ascent to our previous level. We saw no more of the attacker and 10 minutes later we turned to port and were heading for the Cherbourg Peninsular. At that moment Red came on the intercom "Enemy aircraft on the port beam - dive port. GO". We opened fire simultaneously and the fighter broke off the attack without firing, vanishing into the darkness. By now I was sweating like a pig. I continued to search the skies intently, up and down, left and right, rotating the turret as I did so. The intercom came on again, but this time it was Frank speaking from the bomb aimers position "Left, steady, left, left, left, steady, steady – leaflets going"

The bulk of the packages of leaflets were stowed in the fuselage, not dropped from the bomb bay. Harry had been busy shovelling them down the flare chute on instructions from Frank, while a number of bundles kept in the nose were pushed out by Frank from his position. By now all the leaflets had been despatched, and we were much closer to the centre of Cherbourg and, thankfully, the coast. The flak was frightening, and we dived starboard and headed for England. We had one more shock just after crossing the coast when we thought that another attack was developing. Gradually the dim shape of the other aircraft came closer, then in the faint light of the flak barrage I recognised the nose down attitude of another Whitley. Gradually we drew away from each other and flew on in relative peace. Some 90 minutes later we touched down at Abingdon with our first operation at an end. After the debrief we went back to the mess for our flying meal, afterwards congregating in the bar for a few drinks and a natter with the other crews, all of whom had returned physically if not mentally unscathed.

CHAPTER 8
HEAVY CONVERSION UNIT - RAF RUFFORTH

Two days later we were on our way for what would be the final stage of our training before going on to our squadrons for operations. We had been posted for ops to 4 Group, and would therefore be flying in Halifaxes. Our new posting was to be No.1663 H.C.U. (Heavy Conversion Unit) at Royal Air Force, Rufforth, just outside York. Here we should be converting on to Halifax bombers, quite different aircraft from the old Whitley.

Back to Yorkshire we went. This time it was well into winter and we had on/off days of snow and sunny frosty weather. The Station was comfortable, and about four miles from York, a city that we all liked. There was lots of entertainment there including that Mecca of all aircrew, Betty's Bar, as well as the Cliffton Rooms, a very well appointed dance hall. At this time we did not know to which squadron we should be posted, but in 4 Group most squadrons were within easy reach of York, a fact that pleased us immensely.

We commenced our conversion on to four engine bombers. At first we had some problems, particularly Red and myself. All our recent training had been done on Frazer Nash gun turrets, whereas the Halifaxes were equipped with turrets manufactured by Boulton & Paul. These turrets were much roomier than the Frazer Nash which was welcome, but the firing and turret control system which worked off a joy stick was quite different to what we had been used to. This central control in the rear turret moved on a type of universal joint around 360 degrees. The gun "fire" trigger was a button on top of this column. After a week or so, despite these differences, we became used to them. I suppose, if we continued to use these turrets, we should have become completely at home with the system and not wished to change back again to the Frazer Nash.

We soon settled into our new unit, and were engaged in similar exercises to those that we had had at Abingdon though at this Station we were not required to go on another leaflet raid. During our stay at Rufforth there was one particularly amusing incident which always remained in my

View from a Birdcage

memory. Ten of us were billeted in the usual Nissen about five minutes walk from the Sergeants Mess. We all got on very well together except for one minor problem. One of the residents, Bob, found it impossible to get out of bed in the morning at the required time. He usually had to miss breakfast in the Mess, arriving very dishevelled for morning parade. Whilst it was true that his continuous late arrival did not affect us personally, it was none the less considered a bit of a slur on all occupants of the billet. One day the rest of us decided that something would have to be done about it, and secretly made plans for what we hoped might be a cure. We had, of course, tried all normal methods of persuasion in endeavours to get him up, ranging from a wet sponge, to tipping him out of bed – all to no effect.

Following our secret plan we had to wait for a few days, but finally when we got up in the morning we saw that the time was right. During the night it had snowed heavily and outside in the fields it was eight inches deep. At a pre-arranged signal, eight of us grasped his bed and carried it and him out of the hut and into the middle of a large rutted field. There we dumped him and walked back to the Mess for breakfast with his pleas and curses ringing in our ears! I cannot begin to imagine what it must have been like to walk back, barefooted and in pyjamas, through eight inches of snow! The lesson was well taken and thereafter we had no further trouble with our slothful friend.

Our stay at Rufforth was only to be about fourteen days in all, and the time was drawing to an end. Our last week was a very sad time for the crew. On Tuesday we had just landed from an exercise when we were told that one of the other crews, engaged on the same exercise, had crashed on the outskirts of York. Everyone was killed. One of my closest friends, Sid the rear gunner, was in the crew, and I had the sad duty of being included in the Guard on his coffin at York Railway Station where we were to meet his parents coming up from London to claim his body for burial. In due course we loaded the flag covered coffin onto the train. This was the first time that we had experienced tragedy during the whole of our flying training.

There was no more flying to be done, except for Duggie. He had already passed out as a qualified pilot of the Halifax, and it was customary when the crew had reached the end of their training for the pilot of each crew to be given first hand experience by being sent to an operational squadron in the Group where he would do one bombing raid as "second dickey" (reserve pilot). Amid much excitement and trepidation, Duggie left us and went with the other pilots for the operation, which we subsequently learned was on Berlin. The next morning, as he hadn't returned from the Squadron, we carried on with some ground training. In mid morning the Adjutant sent for us and imparted the appalling news that Doug had been posted missing from the raid.

At first we couldn't take it in. Less than twenty four hours before the seven of us had been excitedly planning our new life on the Squadron to which we would have been posted. We had been looking forward to being on ops, at long last, and now we were a headless crew with an uncertain future. Later that day we were all sent on 14 days leave and were told that on our return a batch of new pilots would be waiting for us. To our very great relief we learned that our crew would not be split up – rather that we should get a new pilot. What a great relief this was! It was only when we were with the Adjutant that we were told that two other pilots from Rufforth had gone missing on the same raid.

Two weeks later we reported back from leave and commenced the task of mutually agreeing who was to be our new skipper which meant that both the new potential pilot and the crew were each satisfied with their choice. The Royal Air Force had a very good method of achieving this in the right atmosphere. There was nothing so mundane as arbitrarily appointing pilots to crews. It was arranged that all spare crews and pilots met on what was more or less a social occasion. Drinks were available and we all milled around together, chatting up prospective pilots and they potential crews. To the best of our ability we sized each other up during the occasion, and the modest drinking taking place released inhibitions, making the task much easier and more pleasant. Bearing in mind the vital need of having personalities that did not clash, this was an excellent way of crewing up, and largely forestalled the likelihood of troubles in the crew of seven when on operations. Such trouble would have been unthinkable, and highly dangerous.

After this very pleasant social evening was at an end, a prospective new pilot, Emmie (Emile), and the rest of the crew had mutually agreed to join forces. Prior to this decision Emmie, who was commissioned in the rank of Flight Lieutenant had said that he liked the thought of us as his prospective crew. However he had to say that during his earlier time as Staff pilot (he had by then done many hundreds of hours flying as an instructor) with Training Command, he had made many useful contacts in Bomber Command – none more to his liking than one with 8 Group Pathfinder Force. As a result, he had been provisionally accepted for duties as a bomber pilot in 8 Group, and had been promised a transfer posting to that Group as soon as he had a crew. Emmie was quite determined to join the P.F.F., thus if he were to be our captain, we had to be agreeable and be prepared to fly as Pathfinders. Needless to say we all jumped at the offer, and were thrilled at the opportunity to fly in Lancasters of the Pathfinder Force.

In this new crewing up process there was one sad decision to be made. Emmie had brought with him from Training Command, Roy, a wireless operator with the rank of Warrant Officer. Roy had already done a tour of operations in the Middle East and was coming back to start his second tour. This meant that our present Wireless Operator, Hank, was surplus to requirements. Because of this dilemma, finalising our decision was deferred until we could all discuss it in the billet that night. As it happened, the decision was made with no great difficulty. Hank himself made it for us by saying that he had no desire to go into Pathfinders. Although at the time his feelings had seemed to be honestly expressed, I could never really decide whether he was letting us off the hook, or was genuine in his desire to stay in 4 Group.

The following morning we officially became a crew, and commenced a final week of training at Rufforth. Although in due course we should be flying in Lancasters, Emmie was still required to qualify on four engine aircraft, as well as to get used to us as a crew and us with him. The week passed quickly enough and we soon began to appreciate Emmie's piloting skills, borne of his long experience as a Staff pilot. As it happened in this final week we had one experience that tested us as a crew. During a Navex we had returned from a fairly long trip, and were approaching Rufforth for landing when the port outer engine caught fire. With no problem or panic, the engine was successfully feathered, the Graviner (fire extinguisher in the engine bay) was operated and the fire extinguished after which a perfectly normal landing was made on three engines. As it happened, at no other time during training trips, or on operations, did we have an engine on fire, though on three occasions during ops we had single engine failures. On two of these occasions the engine failures took place whilst we were on our way to the target. Fortunately the Halifax functioned well on three engines. Climbing speed and height were affected to a certain amount, otherwise flying was uneventful, though it was physically a lot harder on the pilot because of the extra effort needed to keep the aircraft flying correctly. Allowance had to be made for the additional drag to one side due to having only one engine functioning on one wing and the dead weight of the other. Although the aircraft could be trimmed partly to offset the imbalance, it was still more of an effort to fly the Halifax.

By the weekend our posting to 8 Group had come through and we had to report to the Pathfinder Force Night Training Unit at Royal Air Force Warboys, near Huntingdon. We were to be there for fourteen days, our principal task being to convert to Lancaster bombers. This was a most enjoyable and exciting experience, and flying in this aircraft after the Halifax was not unlike comparing a sports car to a family saloon. There was not a lot of difference between the performance of the two aircraft, though the Lancaster did have the edge in speed and height attained. What was noticeable was the very superior manoeuvrability of the Lanc. To us she was indeed "The Queen of the Skies". During our stay we had a lot of training to do, comprising mainly of navigation exercises. First class navigation was the prime requirement of a Pathfinder crew. Frank was pleased to find that as well as being the bomb aimer, he was now Nav.II, resulting in him becoming Ernie's full time assistant. We also had quite a lot of bombing exercises over the Wainfleet range in Lincolnshire. These bombing exercises were usually combined with air firing exercises en route to Wainfleet. The change to Lancs brought us another personal bonus; we were back in Frazer Nash turrets. We were worked very hard by the Group to bring us up to the high standards they required, and we heaved a sigh of relief when we had finished our training and were initiated as a Pathfinder crew.

Towards the end of our stay at Warboys we had a wonderful evenings entertainment when Major Glenn Miller and his band visited the Camp. The theatre was filled to overflowing, leaving no room for dancing. However, who worried – all we wished to do was listen to this fantastic band, which we did until the small hours. Sadly, not very long after Glenn Miller was to go missing on a flight and no trace of the light aircraft that he was in was ever found. One great item of news reached us before we left Warboys. This was that Duggie was safe in a P.O.W. camp, having successfully baled out during the raid on Berlin. (Shortly after the end of the war he visited us and we had a great celebration. He was well but had lost a lot of weight.)

Finally the day came for us to leave Warboys, and we were told that we had been posted to No.35 Squadron R.A.F. Gravely which was just a few miles down the road. However, later that same day, this posting was changed to No.635 Squadron at R.A.F. Downham Market, Norfolk This Squadron had just been formed, and some of the crews from R.A.F.

Gravely had already been posted there to form a nucleus of operational crews. We were to be amongst the new boys at Downham Market when we arrived at 08.300 hrs the following morning. As our skipper Emmie had received an invitation to attend a big party at R.A.F. Mildenhall the night before our move, we were given permission to break our journey there and fly the short distance to Downham Market in the morning. We took off after dark, arriving at Mildenhall within twenty minutes. Emmie, Ernie, Frank and Red went off to the Officers Mess, the rest of us being invited to the Sergeants Mess where there was also a big party in full swing. This went on until 2 am, when rather shakily, and amid much singing of bawdy songs, "Cats on the Roof Top" etc, we staggered off to a rather bleak Nissen hut on the edge of the camp. Take off was at 8 am; we were awakened at 6.30 am, and went to the mess for an early breakfast, afterwards walking across the airfield to where our Lanc was parked. The previous night we had learned that only half of the Squadron were at the parties, the other half being on operations. They had landed after we had gone to bed, but we were too far gone to have heard them. We saw, in the dim light, that there were many more additional aircraft on the dispersals than there had been on the previous evening – the extra aircraft being those that had been on ops. In the distance one of the Lancasters had a crowd around it, and we wandered over to see what all the excitement was about. To my horror, I saw that the crowd were gathered around the rear turret – what little of it remained. The previous night this Lanc had suffered a sustained attack by a night fighter and had suffered considerable damage. The rear gunner and most of his turret had been shot away by cannon shells, and the tidying up process was now going on. It was a miracle that the aircraft ever got back, let alone landed, particularly as a large part of one of the fins and rudders was missing. Not the best of introductions for a crew about to commence operations!

Shortly afterwards the rest of the crew arrived, looking a little bit jaded, and we took off for 635 Squadron, Downham Market where we were surprised to learn that we had yet more training to get through before we could even be considered up to Pathfinder Force standards. After another seven days of continuous flying exercises, both day and night, we were satisfactorily passed out and were ready for our first operational trip, in the lowest grade of "Supporters". We geared ourselves for what was to be "The big one"!

We had had one rather scary trip during this latest training. We were engaged in a navigational training exercise that took us up to Scotland.

Chapter 8 - Heavy Conversion Unit - RAF Rufforth

The weather was foul, thick cloud from 1,000 feet to 20,000 feet. There was just an occasional break but rarely a sight of the ground. Two thirds of the trip had been successfully accomplished with the aid of Gee and H_2S_2, when an electrical fault developed making them both u/s. The rest of the trip had to be done on dead reckoning and when we were within about 30 minutes of base I was startled to hear Emmie's voice on the intercom saying "Balloons, Balloons". Fortunately, we had come into a clearish patch of sky, though the ground was still invisible, only to find ourselves in the middle of a balloon barrage which we subsequently learned was from Birmingham. From my view, looking to the rear, I had ghastly visions of balloons whipping by, seemingly just off our wing tips. One balloon cable would have sufficed to have brought us down, probably taking a wing off in the process. Somehow, Emmie did his usual marvellous job of piloting, and after a few minutes of high drama we had left the barrage behind, unscathed but mentally scared to death.

Myself, the 'sprog' Sergeant in 1943.

CHAPTER 9
COMBAT

The great day for our first operation arrived, and at briefing we learned that our target was a rail junction at Ottignies in Belgium close to the German frontier. One's first trip bears a charisma that keeps it apart from all subsequent trips. In the event it was cloudless with a moon which didn't do anything for our nerves. As it happened we were spared fighter attacks, though our first experience of near accurate flak over the Belgium coast in the vicinity of Dunquerque was nerve shattering. As it transpired, no burst were dangerously close, though we did have a few small flak holes in the fuselage. Fortunately all the damage was cosmetic. All in all, the experience provided a fillip for our morale, and on our return we felt like seasoned veterans! This raid was considered successful, subsequent photo reconnaissance showing that the rail junction was out of use.

Despite all the excited chatter after the trip, Roy was quiet and said very little. It was not until the following morning that we were shattered by his comments and opinion with regard to that trip. As it happened, this conversation took place in our billet. Since Roy, Harry and myself were senior NCOs at the time we were quartered together. The rest of the crew were commissioned and billeted in Officers' quarters. There were therefore only the three of us together at the time of this discussion. Roy calmly informed us that as the only operationally experienced member of the crew, he considered that Emmie would not make a good operational pilot. His opinion shattered us since inexperienced though we were, we felt extremely happy with Emmie's captaincy. On his first trip, when things had got sticky, he never lost his calmness and this very naturally came over to us, inspiring confidence when it was most needed. In addition to his undoubted excellence and skill as a pilot we all liked him as a person.

We tried desperately to talk Roy out of his (we felt) unreasonable personal assessment of Emmie, but to no avail. We were sad to be losing the comradeship of Roy, a man that we all personally liked. Later that morning he raised the subject with the Skipper. In view of the

Chapter 9 - Combat

vital necessity of having the entire crew of seven people without any personality clashes, the Royal Air Force allowed any member of aircrew to opt out of his crew should he not be able to fly with them all amicably. This privilege, of course, also extended to the Captain who could ask that a member, or members, of his crew be replaced.

The result of Roy's decision, despite further talks with the whole of the crew, were negative. He was subsequently relieved of his duties with us and sent on seven days leave. Upon his return he was posted to a new crew but he did only one trip with this crew (we were on the same operation). Roy's aircraft failed to return and he was posted "Missing", and subsequently "Killed". Our future success was unknown, but it was an ironic quirk that we should go on to complete, with God's help and a very much above average run of luck, 62 operations. At the end of the war in Europe we were the oldest and most experienced crew on the Squadron.

In my turret. Taken before take-off and ready for action.

View from a Birdcage

*The crew; No. 1.
From left to right:
Pilot Flt Lt Emile
Mange, Navigator
F/Off Ernie Mawson,
B/Aimer/ Nav II
F/off Frank Jackson,
W/Operator W/O Tim
Redfern, M/U Gunner
P/O "Red" Winch,
R/Gunner Sgt Jack
Catford, Flt Engineer
Sgt Harry Wooding*

Crew No. 2 As above except in centre of picture- Flt Lt Jack Allen.

56

CHAPTER 10
MUNICH

The mid January day in 1945 was cold and cheerless; the bleak wind whined and sighed over the fens and through the camp. I was sitting in front of a brightly burning fire in the Officers Mess day - dreaming. The months past had seen us slowly move on from being a "sprog" crew to one of the senior crews on the Squadron. By now we had completed many operations over enemy territory. Luck had not deserted us, though at times it had been a close thing, leaving us mentally scarred but still with an overwhelming desire to complete our two tours of operations. Our day to day life had become most enjoyable when some months previously, Harry, our Flight Engineer, and myself had received our commissions; thus we now all used the same Mess and slept in the same Billet, other than Emmie who as a senior officer was billeted elsewhere. Another source of great satisfaction was that we had each been awarded "gongs". I awoke fully at the same time recalling that as it was Wednesday there was at least one important function that beckoned, and would be well patronised by the Squadron. This was the dance in the Town Hall at Downham Market, It was always a very popular and crowded affair, and towards the end of the evening, as a result of the closing of the pubs, dancing would become almost an impossibility. Nonetheless, the relaxation and companionship afforded by this gathering more than compensated for the discomfort of the crowded floor.

These rather pleasant trends of thought were abruptly terminated by the arrival of Red, my mid upper gunner, announcing himself in his usual hearty manner by administering a hefty whack on my back, accompanying this by a verbal warning that "The war is on again tonight"! We had operated on the previous night, and this had buoyed up my hopes for the evening outing that I had promised myself. Well that was definitely a non-runner now, so nothing to do except to make the mental adjustment required and hope for better luck next time. "Flying meal at 15.30 and briefing at 16.30" said Red, "see you back at the billet."

In view of the now pending trip, I did not make the usual obligatory

View from a Birdcage

call at the Gunnery Section, deciding that the additional ground training of aircraft recognition and night vision exercises, as set out by the Gunnery Leader, should be missed in view of the now more urgent task of going out to the aircraft to check guns, turret and ammunition tanks. I knew that I would almost certainly meet other air gunners engaged on similar checks. Rather than wait for the crew bus, I grabbed my cycle from outside the Mess and pedalled off to the aircraft dispersals, a journey of some two miles. Along I went, right through the domestic site, across the main Downham Market/Swaffham road, and onto the airfield proper. As I passed the various crew sections, I was joined by other members of the Squadron aircrews intent on similar business to my own.

Out on the airfield perimeter track it was a tidy battle against the buffeting wind. Eventually I arrived at Willie's dispersal, and made a quick dive for the ground crew's quarters where I stopped for a chat. They were a splendid bunch of lads and we had the utmost confidence in them and the vital work that they did in sorting out all the problems on our aircraft - Willie. Fred, the corporal i/c greeted me with a more than welcome cup of NAAFI tea and a "wad". He had seen me cycling from afar whilst the NAAFI wagon was serving them. Three other lads formed the ground crew for our aircraft. There was one addition to the crew, Nigger, an enormous black tom cat. He appeared one day, from heaven knows where, and adopted us all. He too was a devotee of NAAFI "wads and char", and at the present time was devouring same on the windowsill. Naturally everybody kept him plentifully supplied with scraps from the mess, hence his enormous size. As to our ground crew, as a small appreciation for the work that they did for us, after every trip we each put a shilling in the kitty (big money in those days!), then once a month or thereabouts we all used to go out to a local pub for a boozy evening.

The ground crew and ourselves were extremely lucky in the dispersal accommodation that we shared with them. Most huts built on aircraft dispersals by the ground crews were made of scrap materials - anything that could be found or scrounged! This largely comprised of old pieces of corrugated iron, scrap timber or even canvas, all gathered from a variety of sources. By great good luck, Willie's hard standing was adjacent to an old derelict farm cottage, and although initially very dilapidated, was soon made waterproof and put in good order by ground crew. In addition, we were fortunate in that our rigger was by profession a commercial artist, and thus the cottage was decorated extensively by life size murals, mostly of ladies in various stages of undress.

Chapter 10 - Munich

W for Willie with his aircrew (standing) and groundcrew (seated).

View from a Birdcage

Having finished my refreshments I went outside and put up the harmonizing board behind the aircraft, ready to line up the four Browning machine guns contained in my rear turret. The harmonizing board was approximately 4ft. square and was mounted on an easel. In the top left hand corner of this board was inscribed a large "X". In each of the other three corners there was a large "O". Having set up the board the correct distance behind the turret I got into the aircraft, clambered down the back of the fuselage and climbed into the turret. Having centralised the turret with the manual lever provided for such purposes, I lined up the guns approximately with the marks on the board, and proceeded to remove the breech blocks from each of the guns so that I was able to look down each barrel in turn, thus looking out of the back of the aircraft towards the board. By now one of the ground crew had come out of the cottage to assist me, and under my directions he moved the board slightly from side to side until I lined up the barrel of the "master gun" with the "X" on the board. This was the top left hand gun which could not be moved on its mounting. Having now correctly aligned the master gun, I then set about lining up the remaining three guns by gazing down each barrel in turn, moving the guns where necessary until I could see the appropriate "O"s. Each of the three remaining guns had individual adjustment rings, and having set the master gun properly it was therefore possible to line up the remaining guns correctly. The correct harmonizing of the guns meant that when all the guns were firing in unison, the resulting cone of fire would converge at 400 yards behind the aircraft. This distance was the point blank range when aiming at a fighter that was attacking from dead astern at that distance. This harmonizing drill was required whenever the guns had been used, and indeed it was my normal practice to adjust them after each flight irrespective as to whether or not the guns had been fired. I had found that the continual vibration of the aircraft

Outside my "office".

Chapter 10 - Munich

was sufficient to throw the guns slightly off-centre. At worst, badly harmonized guns in combat could mean the difference between life and death.

Next on the agenda was the cleaning and checking of each individual gun. Armourers did this after every flight, the guns being taken back to the armoury for that purpose. A wise gunner, however, still checked his own guns; this I proceeded to do. By now Harry and Nobby had come out to do there own daily inspections and checks. The NAAFI wagon was on its return trip, so I stopped it and scrounged some more tea for them.

Having finished my work, and with lunch time approaching, I decided to return to the billet for a wash and brush up prior to going on to the Mess. On the way back I stopped at the Gunnery section to check up on any "gen", and to sign the gunnery order book. There was the usual small gaggle of gunners gossiping, in the main about likely targets for tonight's operation. This would certainly remain a close secret until navigation and main briefing although it had been known for certain crafty members of aircrew to find out, by devious means, what fuel load was to be carried. Because of the time and work involved in refuelling the sixteen aircraft on tonight's operation, refuelling would have commenced early – as soon as operations had been ordered. Knowing the fuel load, and the normal consumption of fuel by the Lancaster, it was possible to make an inspired guess. Even so, the margin for error was very great, since to be accurate it was also necessary to know the weight of the bomb load to be carried, and this could not easily be ascertained.

I left the billet shortly afterwards, and then on to the Mess where I was one of the early arrivals so that I was able to lunch in the first wave, afterwards securing a comfortable seat in the ante room where I devoured a few newspapers before settling down to a brief snooze. After a while, the buzz of conversation awakened me. I popped into the bar for a quick beer, and then collecting my bike I returned to the billet once more. On my return I found that Red, Nobby and Harry were already there, together with Colin, an Australian pilot, and Don, his navigator. A lively game of pontoon was in progress so I joined the school, having an enjoyable hour, and coming out evens. Creeping over to my bed I managed to get in another small kip before Red rudely awakened me. Taking the odd snooze whenever the opportunity presented itself had become a way of life with us since we never knew, until sometimes quite late in the day when we should be operating and more importantly, where we should be going and how long the trip would be. The operation that we had been on the

Ready to load up. Munitions came in all shapes and sizes. Here we see an example of a 12,000 lb 'blockbuster' on the main trolley and a 1,000 lb and 500 lb bomb on the smaller trolley.

previous night had commenced quite early and the target had not involved us in too deep a penetration of the Third Reich so we had therefore been back soon after midnight and in bed shortly after 1 a.m. Because of this, we were only an hour late getting up this morning. Tonight's operation might prove to be a lot longer, hence the grabbing of shut eye whenever possible.

Regardless of snow 4000lb bombs being loaded.

I got off the bed in time to make my first change of clothing before going back to the Mess for the flying meal at 15.30. This wasn't all that long after lunch, but we had to be prepared for anything up to twelve hours before the next meal, assuming always that there would be a next meal! By this time, all the crew with the exception of Emmie had joined us in the billet. Ernie and Frank our nav team, both New Zealanders, were once again very busy discussing the likely target. Harry, Nobby and Red had already changed. Emmie was living in the Rectory of the little Norman church which was on our camp. All senior officers were billeted there.

The weather looked like remaining pretty cold, so I decided to wear the whole works. Experience had taught me that if in doubt wear everything. Even in what we would call moderate flying temperatures, the rear turret was the coldest spot imaginable. On a so called warm trip, at this time of year the temperature would probably be at least 10 degrees below zero at 10,000 feet. Whilst on a cold trip, at our operational height of 20/22,000 feet, it could easily reach 50/60 degrees below. Out came my glamour pants, a long silk and wool garment which stretched from ankles to armpits and was followed by a long sleeved vest of the same material. Next came my operational shirt – an opened necked civilian version. This

View from a Birdcage

Outside our billet at Downham Market. Left to right (standing); Don Swaffield - Navigator, Alan Brown - Navigator, Frank Jackson - Bomb Aimer and Nav II, Doug Boards - Pilot, Harry Wooding - Flt Engineer, "Red" Winch - M/U Gunner.
Seated are Selwyn Booth - Bomb Aimer and Nav II and Colin Ottway - Pilot.

garment was my sole concession to superstition, and I had worn it on every operation that we had so far done. The shirt should really have been consigned to the salvage bin long ago and extreme manoeuvrability was required to don the garment. With much loving care, this was eventually accomplished, to the usual chorus of jeers and laughter from the rest of the crew. Great raggers, my crew and I responded by hurling a handful of coke cinders at the jeer leader. In the resulting melee, my precious shirt gained yet another rent. Finally, I sorted out a long sleeved woollen coat and donned same, stuffing the pockets with a few personal escape aids and sweets, then into my battle dress and the first stage of dressing was completed.

By now it was close on 15.30, and with a final check to see that nothing had been forgotten we all trooped out and cycled off to the Mess for our eggs and bacon. Upon arrival the meal had commenced, so wasting no time we got down to the serious business of enveloping a huge meal which would have to last us, almost certainly, to the small hours of the following day. It was a somewhat hurried meal and all to soon we were interrupted by the Tannoy, announcing that the crew buses were waiting outside the Mess. Regretfully we spilled outside and clambered onto the

Chapter 10 - Munich

waiting transport. The ride to the Briefing Room was not very far, and a few minutes later we arrived and streamed into the long lecture hall, having first been checked into this Holy of Holies by the S.P.s guarding the doors.

Inside it was quite an imposing edifice with its many chairs and tables arranged down the hall in long columns. Each crew sat at the table that was marked with their aircraft identity. The walls were adorned with many drawings, charts and sundry other items, including of course, the Ministry of Information posters which urged us to "Be like Dad - Keep Mum"! At the end of the hall above a dais, but at present hidden by a curtain, was a huge operational map of Europe that remained concealed until the Station Commander arrived and opened the briefing. An intriguing map this, which would show, first and foremost, our target for tonight's operation with ribbons showing our routes from base to target and back to base again. The outward and return journeys were always different; also shown on the map were all well known flak and searchlight defended areas, red areas denoting flak and blue areas searchlights. These red and blue areas were usually together, the outer ring being searchlights and the inner flak batteries, with very occasionally a flak or searchlight battery on its own.

The defence areas varied in density depending to a large extent upon the importance of the potential target and target area. Large cities and important industrial complexes naturally had a very heavy concentration with the smaller targets being less heavily defended. The defence areas around the Ruhr were terrific and stretched in one continuous belt covering many hundreds of square miles in area; hence our ironic name for it –"Happy Valley"! The route in and out of enemy territory naturally took these areas into consideration, and whenever possible it was planned to avoid or skirt these areas for as long as feasible, or until such times as the bombers were running up over the target when things usually livened up to a considerable degree!

If the route to the target were to be direct, the journey time could in some cases be halved but the losses were likely to go up by 100% or more. By skilful routing we tried to make the German defences very uncertain until the last possible moment where the target was to be. In fact the last turning point was often an equal distance from two major cities. Occasionally of course the Germans made an inspired guess that worked out! I remember our trips to Stettin and Lubeck, both in north east Germany, in the Baltic coast region. On both occasions we were routed out over the east coast of England, and then to the extreme north of Denmark where we turned starboard and stooged down for what seemed hours over the Kattegat and Skaggerak, coming into the target from the north. A similar route was used for subsequent raids in that area of Germany. On both of these trips the distance travelled was almost twice the distance of the direct A to B route. Exceptionally, when we were doing the buzz bomb sites which were mostly in the Pas des Calais area, we went direct since very little enemy territory had to be crossed. These buzz bomb sites were mostly raided in daylight. It was a strange feeling to see beneath us the flying bombs on their way to London and the south east. On such trips our height was not great, except when crossing the coast of France, and there were occasions when my fingers itched to poop off at these flying bombs, many of which were within range. However, the burning desire had to be stifled because if I were lucky enough to score a direct hit, the resultant blast could easily have destroyed us.

Just as much care had to be taken on our routes out of the U.K. Allowances had to be made for hundreds of bombers to blend smoothly together and in the right place. The most commonly used exits for the bombers from this country were over Southwold and Orford Ness in East Anglia. Another well used route involved the bomber stream meeting over Reading and exiting over Beachy Head.

We were now all seated and the briefing commenced. As the curtains were drawn, eyes were strained to pierce the tobacco smoke in order to see the map, where our target was to be ....it was Munich. This would be a very long trip, but at least we hadn't operated on this target before. A new name in our log book was always welcome. I noted that our crew were shown on the Battle Order as being delegated deputy Master Bomber. Hopefully, and for the best of reasons, the Master Bomber would not get the chop, in which case we shouldn't be called upon to be the last aircraft home! I pondered to myself wondering what the defences would be like. The red and blue areas around the target looked very ominous. I wondered also if we should have any trouble with fighters or if it would prove to be a dicey target, generally? Ah well, time would tell. At this moment the C.O. moved to the front of the dais and the briefing commenced.

Having given us the plan and type of attack, the C.O.'s place was taken by an Intelligence Officer. He supplied us with the most up to date information on the defences, what the importance of the target was in terms of manufactured material – usually of a war like nature – and gave to us a general idea of the importance of the target to the German war effort.

Chapter 10 - Munich

It was now the turn of the Navigation Leader. As we were a Pathfinder Squadron, this briefing was particularly thorough, right down to the last minute detail. The aircraft nav team always had an earlier additional briefing prior to the main briefing, since the amount of planning and preparation required of them was quite extensive. Ernie and Frank were now working hard on the finishing touches to their charts adding further details and information now being supplied. Other than when on the bombing run, or manning the front turret, Frank worked with Ernie at the chart table. Next came the Bombing Leader who gave details of the target indicators, (coloured flares with which the Pathfinders marked the target, thus enabling the following main force bombers to aim correctly) flares and markers that we should be carrying. We were also given details of the bomb load which usually would be about 75% of the total load. The Signals Leader now supplied his usual mine of information, eagerly taken down by Nobby. Emmie also made notes on this part of the briefing for his own benefit. A short talk was given by the Engineering Officer, with emphasis on the amount of fuel carried, and the times for changing over the various fuel tanks – very vital in maintaining the trim of the aircraft. This was of particular interest to Emmie and Harry, the latter being responsible for the actual changeover.

Next came the Met Officer, and it was soon apparent that the weather was not going to be particularly pleasant. Very thick cumulus nimbus clouds (thunder clouds) were expected over a large part of the route, other than in the early part of the journey, and in places they would be solid right up to 30,000ft. or higher with the icing index high. The only hope offered for the outbound trip was a possibility of cloud clearance in the vicinity of the target. We did not particularly relish such a clearance at this time since we suspected that the Munich area might prove to be a hot bed of night fighters. Altogether the forecast was not at all to our liking. After fog, cu-nim cloud formation was the worst possible type of weather condition in which to fly. Apart from the incredible buffeting that we would receive, the trouble would mainly be severe icing. If the clouds were as thick as forecast, they were likely to persist and would probably worsen until such time as we might find a clear lane between two layers of cloud in which to fly, or until we could get right out of it. All the exposed moving parts of the aircraft would build layer upon layer of ice causing the aircraft to be very sluggish in responding to the controls. The propellers too would build up their quota of ice that would tend to add to the general vibration. Fortunately when the propellers iced up, it usually happened that after a

View from a Birdcage

certain thickness had formed the ice would disintegrate and be thrown off in lumps. On the debit side, these flying chunks of ice have been known to break through the Perspex panels in the pilot's and bomb aimer's side panels!

In addition to all these troubles, the pilot's windscreen would most probably become opaque because of the thickness of the ice formation. If this occurred he would have to fly blind, that is on instruments only. Anti-icing devices were fitted to the pilot's panel, but when the icing was really severe these aids could not always cope. The Perspex on the gun turrets also became opaque, though chiefly on those panels which faced into the slip stream; some panels therefore would remain reasonably clear, sufficiently to be able to see out of them. This problem on the rear gun turrets was solved when it was decided that the rear gunner would only have Perspex above his head and in the side of his turret. Thus in the front of the turret – that is, looking straight out of the back – there was nothing at all and the gunner looked straight out into the void. This absence of Perspex was laughingly referred to as the "clear vision" panel! This was common to all aircraft of the Pathfinder Force and was eventually adopted by some Squadrons on main force. There was one very great advantage to the absence of this panel. Despite regular polishing of the Perspex screen by gunners on the ground, it was all too easy to miss an odd spot, and as a result during some operational trips it was not unknown for the gunner to imagine that the spot was an enemy fighter at extreme range. So long as this error went un-noticed, the gunner might be oblivious of a genuine fighter attack developing from another quarter.

Another problem of flying in cu-nim was that there would almost certainly be electrical storms which could be most unpleasant. The interference from such storms made radio reception pretty hopeless at times. Finally, the turbulence in this cloud formation could cause an aircraft to jump about in a most erratic manner. One minute it would be flying along reasonably steadily, and in the next minute it would be thrown about as if it were a model plane. The many tons of weight counted for nothing in the up and down draughts of a cu-nim. During such periods we should be twisting, shaking and shuddering, with control of the aircraft only maintained by the pilot using every ounce of his strength, often with the need of assistance from the Flight Engineer. Altogether this was a most unpleasant experience suffered by us on several occasions.

It was strange that during the quite extensive flying that we did during our training, the pilots avoided cu-nim like the plague; we would

Chapter 10 - Munich

fly round it, or under it, but never through it. It was rarely possible to fly over the tops since they were normally at 30,000ft or more, a height far beyond the scope of most aircraft other than some fighters. In fact, standing instructions on the Training Squadrons made it quite clear to pupil pilots that there was to be no flying at all in such formations. When we commenced operational flying we learnt to our great surprise that if cu-nim cloud was on our route, or encountered unexpectedly, we should avoid it if possible. In the event of such action being impossible, we were to go right through it! In other words, the most important thing was that the raid must go on, as planned, regardless of risk or discomfort. There was once an occasion when we were on a raid and we taxied out to the take off point in the most torrential rain, with deafening claps of thunder and fork lightning everywhere. When we arrived at the holding position we waited there for 15 minutes. We were already for an abort, and making plans for a jolly evening when we returned to our billets, when, to our surprise, we got a green from the caravan, and the squadron took off as planned, albeit 20 minutes late.

Occasionally, if we were very lucky, it was possible to climb above the cloud into relatively calm air and no further icing. More frequently it went to such a height that this action was impossible and we had to fly through it, hoping at the most for a clear patch here and there.

Tonight's forecast at least made me happy that I had donned my "glamour pants". The Gunnery Leader gave his briefing, emphasising the type of night fighters usually seen in the region of Munich and with whom we could be in combat. We were cautioned because of the very deep penetration tonight to keep extremely vigilant. This was our custom in any case, regardless of the length of the trip. Finally, Flying Control gave us our take off instructions and those for landing on return, together with a note of diversionary airfields available should the weather or any other reason make it impossible to land on our own airfield. This completed the briefing and once more the C.O. mounted the dais, stressed again, the importance of the operation, then wished us good luck and a successful trip.

Now that the briefing was over we still had a fair time to go before going out to the aircraft. While the rest of the crew were working out the remaining details of the trip, including interesting and problematical discussions about the likely opposition and results of the raid, I had one more job to attend to before leaving the room. Wandering to the back of the room I collected my canvas bag ready for filling. Before leaving the

Briefing Room one was required to make a final check of the contents of pockets. It was a strict rule that aircrew should not fly over enemy territory with anything in their pockets, or on their person, which might be of use to German intelligence in the event of the aircraft having crashed and the crew, or some of the crew, being alive and subject to interrogation. The interrogation was conducted by experts in the trade, and the most amazing exports had filtered back of information which had been pieced together from sundry bits and pieces retrieved from aircrew who had been less than careful when emptying their pockets prior to operating.

I emptied my pockets of everything, both likely and unlikely, which might be the means of giving away information. I had already partially emptied my pockets at the billet, but a few remaining items came to light. A collection of small objects including a snapshot taken in Downham of my current girlfriend. These remaining few items went into the canvas bag, which was sealed and my name put on it. It was then stowed away until my return. I now felt security minded and wandered back to join the rest of my crew who were by now ready to leave.

Emmie was handing out the escape aids, each of these being contained in a neat little package about the size of a flat 50 cigarette tin. The contents were quite ingenious. Concentrated glucose and chocolate, condensed milk in a tube, pep tablets (Benzedrene), water purifying tablets, matches, fishing line and hook, safety razor, toothbrush, compass, a small rubber water bottle and soap together with various other small articles of great value if one became an evader in enemy territory. Additionally, a purse was supplied containing the foreign currency of the countries over which we might fly. The purse also contained a silk handkerchief on which were printed maps of the countries on our route, and once more another of the indispensable compasses. We each also carried a personal first aid kit which supplemented the large first aid kits carried on the aircraft. This contained dressings, an ampoule of morphia with syringe and burn jelly together with a pair of specially treated gloves for wearing over badly burned hands – a common combat injury suffered by aircrew.

Of the personal escape aids available to aircrew, none were more important than the secret compasses. These came in an amazing variety. They were contained in brass RAF uniform buttons which unscrewed revealing the secret compass. Some were available concealed in fountain pens. Perhaps the most amusing was the compass comprising of two fly buttons (to be cut off the trousers only when necessary) one button had to be balanced on top of the other, the top button would then swinging round

Chapter 10 - Munich

to point to magnetic north. The cleverest compass was that concealed in a briar pipe. The pipe could be smoked in the normal manner, the smoke by-passing the small concealed compass. One had to unscrew the mouthpiece of the pipe and separate a small section from the middle which revealed the desired object.

The next move which now took place was by bus to the Crew Room. Here we collected our parachutes, harness and Mae West. Our flying clothing was also stored here in heated lockers, each locker being shared by two of the crew. We now collected our chutes, each one being a personal issue. These were kept in a huge permanently heated store. Every day the NCO in charge picked a number of 'chutes at random, and with the WAAF's responsible for packing them, the rip cords were deliberately pulled. Aircrew had access to the 'chute packing room and were encouraged to make visits and watch the girls doing the intricate work. On one occasion, one of the girls pulled my 'chute for me. Result – a perfect opening! I never heard of a parachute failing its test, and we all had complete and utmost trust in the work that the girls did for us.

I began to sort out my flying clothing and commenced to dress. Dressing slowly and carefully was an important point to remember as any haste now meant that with all these clothes on, one perspired very easily, even in winter. Any resulting patches of dampness, as well as being uncomfortable, meant little on the ground whereas once in the air and in very low temperatures, a damp patch almost certainly meant frostbite.

The first item to be put on was the electrically heated suit complete with thin slippers attached - an all in one garment with sleeves down to the wrist. It was not unlike a suit of overalls but had a heating element woven throughout. I normally wore three pairs of gloves - first silk, then electrically heated fleece lined, and finally – leather gauntlets. Two other pairs of gloves were supplied, suede and woollen, but three pairs were as much as I could manage and still get my fingers through the trigger guards of my guns. The electric suit had a lead attached. The plug on the end passed through the layers of clothing when I was finally dressed and connected to a socket in the turret, and thus to the aircraft's electrical system. This was my heating supply. Next I put on a thick woollen sweater that stretched down to my thighs together with a pair of thick thigh length woollen stockings. A Sidcot outer suit followed, with its many feet of zipping, and finally fleece lined black leather and suede flying boots. All that was left to don was the parachute harness and the Mae West, these being left until we were ready to get into the aircraft.

The helmet, together with its attached oxygen mask and intercom set, completed my attire, and with Red, I went over to the test bench to try out my intercom and oxygen mask. In addition, the heated suit was also tested on this bench. Seven amps indicated for the suit, and two amps for the gloves and slippers - that was ok. We were going to be glad of the heat tonight. Feeling very warm and bloated with all this gear on, I walked slowly outside with the rest of my crew, and climbed laboriously onto the Crew bus that was to take us out to Willie. Nobby clambered on with our ration box which contained chocolate, barley sugar, chewing gum, raisins and flasks of coffee, and we were away. The bus lumbered on its way around the perimeter track and turned in towards the various aircraft dispersal points. We had three calls to make, X ray, W Willie and Z Zebra. Our first stop was at X Ray's dispersal point, and the sorting out of bodies, parachutes and various pieces of equipment took place. The last man of this crew dismounted, and with a "Have a good trip" and the old thumbs up sign, they left us and we were on our way to Willie in the next dispersal.

Two of the Ground Crew, Fred and Taffy were waiting and helped us off with the gear. We bade our farewells to the remaining crew and prepared to get into the aircraft to give it its usual thorough ground testing prior to take off in just over an hour's time. Apart from satisfying each member of the crew that his own particular equipment was serviceable, the ground crew were also given time to remedy any snags or unserviceability which might be found to exist or was suspected. In the event of any major problems arising, at least one spare aircraft was on stand by, fully fuelled and loaded up with bombs and markers. Any crew needing it would be quickly whisked around to where it was dispersed.

We all climbed into Willie, moving along to our respective positions. I clambered slowly along inside inspecting the hydraulic system which supplied our turrets with their motive power. I also examined the four big tanks of ammunition which fed back to my turret, as I prepared to enter the rear gunner's position. Getting into it with all my flying clothing on called for a lot of dexterity. First one had to crawl through very narrow bulkhead doors. This was an exceedingly difficult procedure. Finally, and worst of all, I had to twist round onto my back, entering the turret feet first. As I was wearing my full flying outfit, excluding harness and life jacket, this was the time when there was the greatest risk of perspiring that could result in the dreaded damp patch.

In the event of needing my parachute on the trip, the two halves of

Chapter 10 - Munich

the split door in the back of the turret had to be opened with the elbows, the latches being designed to accommodate them. It was then possible to reach back and grab the parachute from the stowage, bring it into the turret and clip it onto the chest harness. If it became necessary to bale out, the rear gunner normally crawled out of his turret (fear adding great dexterity to this exercise), and exited through the door in the starboard side of the aircraft. If this method was impossible, perhaps because of a fierce fire, then having obtained and attached the 'chute, the rear gunner swung the turret round onto the beam, opened the doors and fell out backwards into the void. Because of the very limited space available to the gunner, there were times when it was extremely difficult to get the parachute out of its stowage and back into the turret. Towards the end of the war and because of this problem, rear gunners were issued with pilot type 'chutes. These were permanently attached to one's posterior by a different type of harness and formed a cushion when sitting down. This new issue was very welcome but made the space in the rear turret even more cramped since the addition of a cushion to sit on raised the head even closer to the roof of the turret. My head actually touched the switches in the roof panel and was the cause of the occasional bruise.

Although my position in the aircraft was, without a doubt, the most uncomfortable, the remainder of the crew had many discomforts with which to contend. Starting at Willie's nose, the positions were as follows. In front of and below the pilot was the Bomb Aimer's position. This was occupied by him only when the aircraft was on the bombing run for up to a period of perhaps ten minutes. On rare occasions he also manned the front guns that were also in the nose. On these occasions Frank would move forward from the Navigator's position, where he would have been helping Ernie. He would then squeeze down between the Pilot and the Flight Engineer, climbing down three steps in the nose. On the floor were cushions and pads. When on the bombing run he lay flat on these cushions directly in front of him the bomb sight was mounted over a big panel of plate glass. He was able to look straight down, out of the aircraft, watching the target and aiming point slowly coming up. They were superimposed through the bomb sight. The Pilot would then be given the necessary corrections over the intercom. Mounted on the port side of the fuselage, level with his elbow, was the computing machine that was the brain of the bomb sight. On this "gen" box was set up all the relevant data required, the box doing the rest. Close by were all the electrical bomb release switches. Set in close to the roof of the compartment in front of him was the gun turret containing two Browning machine guns. Usually the Bomb Aimer, but sometimes the Flight Engineer when necessary, manned these guns. The turret was for use mainly against head on attacks. Because of the great closing speed of the Lancaster and a fighter attacking head on, this type of attack was comparatively rare. Only on a few occasions had it been necessary to man this turret and both of our crew members had had a go.

Moving back, up the steps, one came to the "Driver" cabin. Here, in a large seat on the port side sat Ernie, our Captain and Pilot. The seat was adjustable for height and leg space. Spread about the panel in front of the Pilot was a maze of instruments going right across the cockpit panel. The control column was centrally placed in front of him with numerous auxiliary controls and switches on small panels either side of his seat, on the sides of the fuselage and in the roof above his head. The four engine throttles were set in a small console on his right at roughly knee level. The strategic placing of these throttles enabled the Flight Engineer to operate them on take off and landing under the instructions of the Pilot, who on these occasions needed both hands on the flying controls. On the right of the pilot was a narrow gangway in which Harry, the Flight Engineer stood. A collapsible canvas seat was fitted to the starboard side for his use, but he did a lot of moving about and rarely used the seat. The engineer's panel was fitted to the starboard side of the aircraft, slightly behind where he stood. This comprised of a large number of instruments and dials that showed in detail the performance of each of the four engines. Facts and figures taken from these dials were noted on the engineers log at frequent intervals.

Behind the pilot was the Navigation cabin, screened by heavy curtains so that the light that they used would not shine out into the cockpit. This light would have upset the Pilot's night vision as well as being a give away to any prowling night fighters. There was one medium sized table on which the charts were placed, and on which the Navigator's work was done. Above the Navigator's head, and to the front and side of the fuselage were crammed many navigational instruments and gen boxes, mostly radar. Some of the Pilot's instruments were duplicated here, including the air speed indicator and compass. The Master compass was back in the fuselage, close to the entrance hatch.

The Lancaster was equipped with every navigational aid, the two most useful being "Gee" and "H_2S". The former was an excellent aid to pin pointing the geographical position of the aircraft at any time. To do this

Chapter 10 - Munich

it relied on transmissions of radio beams from the United Kingdom. Its only failing was its comparatively limited range. Over the northern area of Europe it was excellent, but as an aircraft got deeper into Germany, starting from about 5 degrees east, it commenced to fade, ultimately becoming unusable. As a comparison, H_2S was completely portable and required no external power or devices. Its picture appeared on the face of a cathode tube in the Navigator's compartment. This picture conveyed an outline of whatever was below the aircraft, not unlike the image on a photographic negative. Its greatest advantage was that it could see through cloud, no matter how thick the cloud was. This was particularly useful for target identification in such conditions, but required skilful interpretation by the Nav team. The equipment's only failing was that eventually the German scientists were able to adapt the equipment fitted on the German night fighters' radar which enabled them to home on any aircraft that were using their H_2S. As a result, the use of this aid was normally restricted to brief periods when necessary in the target area- obviously only when the target was totally obscured by cloud or smoke.

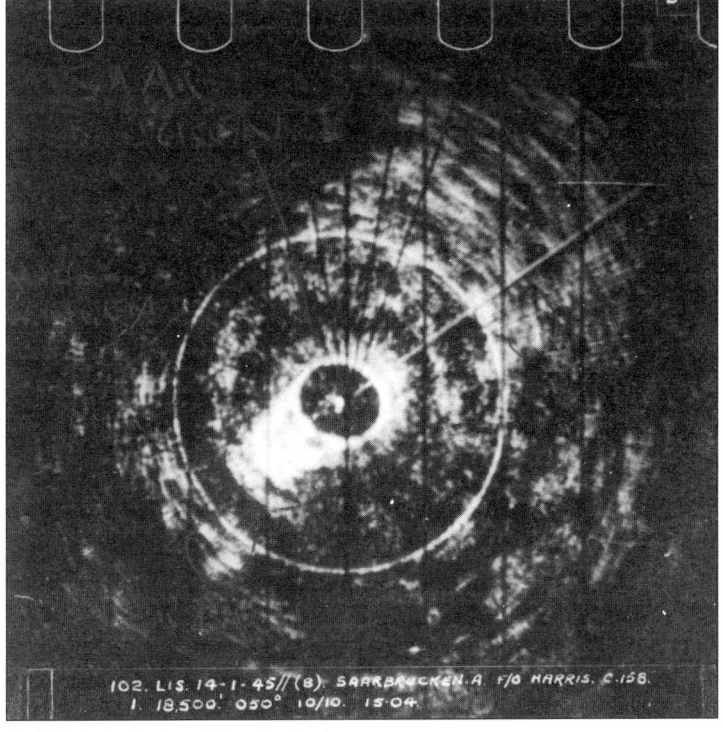

An H_2S photo of a target (Saarbrucken).

The Royal Air Force, knowing that these aids could and did, occasionally malfunction, strictly enjoined Navigators to practice celestial navigation and on each operation the Navigator had to take star shots with his sextant, these shots having to be entered into his log. This was an excellent way to keep the Navigators up to scratch. After the result of the star shots had been noted, Ernie usually checked them against the radar position as shown on Gee or H_2S, and we never knew him to be in error when making the comparison. Occasionally, when the whole of the trip was made in the middle of or under dense cloud, it would not be possible to take this star shot; reliance was then totally on radar.

Moving back along the fuselage, the next position was that of Nobby, the Wireless Operator. He probably had the most comfortable position on the aircraft, though still a little cramped. He had reasonable leg room, with the transmitter/receiver in front of him on a small table on which was mounted the Morse transmission key. There was room, for his logs and papers. On the starboard side was a panel containing most of the fuses of the aircraft's electrical systems. The biggest advantage that he enjoyed was that the aircraft's heating system, which was obtained from the engines, entered the fuselage right where Nobby sat, with the result that he was the only crew member who never suffered from the cold. In fact on occasions he was too hot! Because of this he never had to wear flying clothing, and more often than not was just attired in ordinary battle dress, though he took a flying suit and gauntlets for use in emergencies. The heating system generally was reasonable for those of the crew who were in the front end of the aircraft, though very little heat reached the mid upper air gunner, and none at all to the rear gunner - hence his electrical suit.

Next came the mid-upper gunner. To get to his position from the Wireless Operator it was necessary to climb over a bulkhead and through a door. One had then reached the main body of the aircraft the bomb bay beneath the floor. Immediately on the port side was the rest bed, normally only put to use when a crew member had been injured by flak or fighters. About halfway along was the mid-upper turret. To climb into it a collapsible ladder was lowered and one big step up enabled the gunner to climb into his detachable swing seat. All the instruments and controls in this turret were duplicates, more or less, of those in the tail turret, the main exception being the guns of which there were two instead of four. Also there was no drift scale. The leg space and general comfort were much better than in the rear gunner's position, in addition to which there was a 360° angle of fire with the exception of the small cut out to prevent the gunner from hitting the fins and rudders of his own aircraft! The downward angle of fire was much more limited than that in the rear turret. On training trips I occasionally changed turrets with Red, and the main faults that I found with this turret was the tendency when flying through heavy cloud for the rain or cloud moisture to find its way through the Perspex seams and thence down one's neck. Also, a cutting draught whistled along the fuselage, straight into this turret, via the small of the gunner's back.

There remained only one more position - my turret at the tail end. In the roof was a switch panel which controlled power to the ring sight, also switches for the turret light and heated suit, plus fuses and a Morse signalling set which made communications possible with the rest of the crew in the event of an intercom failure. Right in front of my seat, at eye level, was the gun sight, an optical/electrical instrument. On its screen was formed a reflected image of a ring and bead. The diameter of the ring could be varied to match the wing spans of the attacking aircraft. The sight was equipped with a rheostat control for dimming or brightening the image. This was used at night, or when very dark conditions prevailed, when to have had the full brilliance of the sight would have been ruinous to night vision. Conversely, when flying in daylight the brilliance would be left full on, thus counteracting a brilliant sun or bright sky. Coming up between my legs from the floor was the turret and gun control column. This was equipped with a pair of grips on either side of the column, rather like a pair of very short bicycle handlebars. Movement of these bars controlled the turret rotation and the elevation and depression of the guns. Also attached to these grips were two triggers for the firing of the four Browning .303 machine guns. Additionally, the grips contained two buttons for signalling evasive action to the Pilot should combat manoeuvres be required. These buttons were vital if the intercom was u/s because the Morse signalling lamp set in the roof was far too slow in emergencies. On the starboard side of the turret was the socket for the heating plug of the suit, and a winding handle for the manual operation of the turret should the hydraulics be shot away or damaged. The remaining item was a drift scale and light for the same. When flying in uncertain wind conditions, the navigator would ask me to confirm the degrees of drift and whether from port or starboard.

Either side of me at elbow height were the machine guns, two on each side. Each pair of guns was placed one above the other. The ring sight and my seat were centrally placed between the four guns. The ammunition came up through the floor and thence via a mechanical feed to the guns. With a wander light fitted to a clip in the roof this about completed my various gadgets, though modifications and various improvements were constantly being tested and fitted. Often when I came out to clean the guns and turret, I would find a new switch or control to be tried. The main supply of ammunition was not, as already stated, contained in the turret, but was to be found in the four big tanks, one tank for each gun and situated well back in the fuselage, two on the port side and two on the starboard. Each of the tanks contained approx 2000 rounds of ammunition being mixed, ball, armour pierce, incendiary and trace, the proportions being laid down by Group. This mix could vary depending upon several factors. Running from each tank were four metal tracks along which the rounds of ammunition were pulled by a mechanical and hydraulic feed system. These were fed straight up to the guns whenever the triggers were pulled. If a gun, or one of these tracks, became jammed, an automatic throw out came into action, thus preventing the rounds from piling up in the turret or fuselage, but not stopping the other guns from firing. The used rounds from the rear and mid upper turrets spilled down chutes and out into the slip stream. The front turret did not have this facility and when the guns were fired the gunner finished with spent rounds piled up around his ankles!

Finally, mention must be made of toilet facilities. This was comprised of a chemical closet, the seat of which was fitted with rubber straps to keep it securely closed when the aircraft was involved in violent manoeuvres, a frequent occurrence during most trips. This toilet was located about two thirds along the fuselage, midway between the mid upper and rear gun turrets. With the amount of clothing that I wore, it was quite impossible for me to make use of the toilet. Imagine having to undo harness, webbing, life jacket and five sets of flies! Additionally the risk of exposing oneself to temperatures of 50-60° below zero were too horrifying to contemplate. It was in any case quite impossible for me to leave the turret, since this could be just the time when a fighter attack developed.

As it happened, the toilet was very rarely used by any member of the crew, except very occasionally on training trips. The Pilot, whose presence in his seat was even more essential, usually carried an empty bottle for his relief. In the main, one very consciously attended to the needs of nature immediately before take off, just prior to boarding the aircraft. In view of these problems, it showed a surprising lack of thought on the part of dieticians and cooks flying meals nearly always included baked beans. This meal was the only occasion when this popular item was ignored by the diners.

Having climbed into my turret, I plugged in the intercom and switched on. As yet the set was dead and whilst waiting for the master switch to be operated, I began the turret check. The guns I knew, after the morning check, were OK, but I still had a quick look to make sure. Port guns OK and starboard guns ditto, and all guns on "safe". I continued with my checks the electric ring sight was serviceable and the spare bulb in its container. The numerous switches and fuses were all right as was the signalling set. The ammunition tanks I had checked when first entering the aircraft together with the hydraulic accumulator which powered the turret and ammunition feed. There was now no more that I could do until the engines were running when I would be able to test the turret operating under power.

The intercom came alive and I could hear the crew talking to each other. I heard Emmie call to the ground crew outside "Contact", and heard the first engine cough and splutter, turn over a few revolutions and then stop. Again it began to turn over and after hesitating briefly, burst triumphantly into its familiar roar. The first engine was always started by the trolley accumulator which contained a mass of heavy duty batteries that were always kept fully charged. This was now on the ground in front of the aircraft and operated by one of the ground crew. Leads from this great battery of accumulators were plugged into the port inner engine. This was the first engine to be started because it was fitted with the aircraft's generator. As soon as this engine was started current was generated and the charge went straight into Willie's batteries.

Each engine was started until all were running, warming up ready for a run under full power. Even at their present low revs a minor hurricane was being created to the rear, bending smaller trees and bushes double and raising a mighty cloud of dirt and dust. I was now able to test my turret under power, swinging from port to starboard, elevating and depressing the guns, and testing the fire control. Everything was in perfect order, and with nothing left to do I settled down and waited for Emmie to call me on the intercom.

Shortly afterwards I heard his voice as he called us up in turn. In this way all the intercom points were tested, and we each reported anything requiring attention. The nav team had had one slight snag which they had been able to rectify themselves. Nobby reported all OK in the Wireless Operator's position and I heard my other half, Red, the mid-upper gunner testing and then calling out that everything was on the top line. Now It was my turn "Hello rear gunner, everything OK with you?" I operated the turret, testing for any dead spots in the intercom, then tried out the emergency signalling system and direction indicators, both of which were duplicated on the pilot's panel, so I reported all in order and switched off.

Now the engines, each in turn, were run under full power. The whole aircraft was shuddering, trying to dislodge the chocks under the wheels. Harry was reading off engine, oil and coolant temperatures, also fuel gauge readings and other instruments appropriate to the "stoker" (as he was called). As always, Willie was in fine fettle and one at a time the engines were cut until once more all was peaceful on the dispersal, although away in the distance could be heard the engines of other aircraft whose testing had not ceased.

There was nothing more to be done now, and take off was an hour away, so as one we all got out of Willie and migrated to the ground crew quarters to sit in front of a cheerful wood fire that was burning, and gossip, with perhaps our usual pre-operational game of cards, a habit to which we all subscribed. I congratulated our artistic ground crew member who had decorated old Willies nose. On the outside of the aircraft, on a side panel immediately under the skipper's seat, was a large imaginative painting of one of the ancient Kings of Britain, complete with crown and sceptre and long flowing robes. Over the King's head were inscribed the words "William conquers all". Alongside were painted long rows of bombs, forty five to date. Each bomb represented one operation in which we and our aircraft had taken part. Underneath was a digital sign of derision that we sincerely hoped would be seen by an unsuccessful night fighter! This sign, universally known, was not of a complimentary nature. Shortly afterwards I had the same sign painted under my turret.

By now we had settled down comfortably in front of the fire and were enjoying our game of cards, generally resting until the time came for us to get into our cramped quarters in Willie where we would be incarcerated for the next seven or eight hours. A little later Taffy came in with two cans of NAAFI tea and some wads. I drank sparingly, having no desire to add to my liquid content. The arrival of this refreshment brought the card game to an end. With only fifteen minutes to go, the door opened and the C.O. walked in. He usually came round to each aircraft prior to take off

Chapter 10 - Munich

to satisfy himself that all was in order, and to wish us a good trip. For a minute or two we chatted, then he was off on his next call.

"OK chaps, time to get aboard" said Emmie. A little regretfully, we left the cheerful fire and after a final long drag of our cigarettes and the ritual emptying of bladders, we put on our last articles of wearing apparel. First the Mae West (inflatable life jacket), then on top of everything, the parachute harness, and finally, the leather helmet. Red and myself, being the most heavily garbed members of the crew, helped each other in the final dressing. We now resembled the pre-war Michelin tyre man, and having so much on made it extremely difficult to get one's arms into the life jacket and tie up the numerous tabs, so this help-your-neighbour policy was really essential. We were now ready and once more we went out, climbing for the last time this night into Willie and all set for tonight's operation.

Once again the engines were started. It was getting pretty dark, and added to the crescendo of the engines was the sight of the long blue flames which crept out from behind the exhaust shields. Once we became airborne and the engines settled down to their normal revs, these flames would die down leaving only a faint glow from behind the flame shields. Even so, when over enemy territory it was an uncanny sight in the pitch darkness of a moonless night, to suddenly catch a glimpse of four blue white patches from the engines of another nearby Lancaster or Halifax. There were eight of these exhaust outlets, one on each side of the four engines, but one was rarely in a position to see more than four at any one time. If I ever caught a glimpse of less than four I was extremely suspicious, since to me it meant the possibility of a twin or single engined fighter.

The skipper checked the time with Ernie, and with about four minutes in hand from take off time, he signalled the ground crew to remove the chocks from in front of the wheels, relaxed the brakes and we taxied slowly out of the dispersal onto the perimeter track. Behind us stood the ground crew who had all come out to see us off, giving the thumbs up sign and mouthing, "Good luck". We couldn't hear any words above the noise of the engines, but we knew what they were saying and it made us feel good to have the boys there wishing us a safe return.

Ahead of us were a few aircraft taxiing slowly, while to the rear I could see the remainder of the Squadron effort, stretching back out along the perimeter track, with nav lights gleaming in the dark - cheerful lights, green on the starboard wing tip and red on the port, with nose lights on

View from a Birdcage

A night time start up of a Lancaster.

Run up prior to take off.

"Chocks away".

to show a clear path ahead. Either side of the perimeter track were small bright blue lights sunk in the concrete to guide us along.

Slowly we taxied along and I swung the turret round onto the starboard beam, where I was able to see the first aircraft on the take off position releasing his brakes ready to go. Standing close to the caravan at the beginning of the runway was one of our WAAF Intelligence Officers, Margaret. She always endeavoured to be out on the runway to watch the Squadron take off on operations. As each machine moved along to the take off position she gave them a cheerful wave on their way. It was just another small kindly gesture, and whether she knew it or not, the crews would have missed her if she had not been in her accustomed spot. Numerous other members of the station staff also joined her in waving us farewell.

Suddenly, above the noise of our own and other aircraft, there was a deep intermittent throbbing as G George, the first aircraft off, moved slowly forward. Quickly it came fully into my view, rapidly increasing speed. Soon the tail was up and it roared straight ahead along the runway and off onto its mission. Twice more the sequence was repeated and then it was our turn. Swinging my turret round I locked it centrally. Over the intercom I could hear Emmie giving Harry instructions "2850+9" (revs and boost) and then "All set everybody, we're on our way". The engine revs increased to maximum, and the whole plane shook and strained on the brake-locked wheels. For perhaps 10 seconds this continued, then off brakes and we slowly rolled forward. As we gained momentum, Henry called out the speed to Emmie "80,80,80,90,95,95,95,100,100". As the speed rapidly increased, I waved to the fast disappearing figure of Margaret, and then quickly the tail lifted from the ground. The concrete was flashing by at an amazing rate, and then the tower on the port side came into view then disappeared in a flash. The aircraft felt very light as it was approaching a speed sufficient to become airborne. We bounced lightly; perhaps a couple of times, then the runway leapt away from us as we left the ground. "Undercarriage up" came the Skipper's voice. This order was repeated to Harry, as was the following order for flaps up, and we were on our way. Beacon lights flashed by as we crossed over the airfield boundary, then we swung over to port making a wide sweep of the airfield and commenced to climb.

Downham Market from the air. The airfield can be seen in the top right hand corner.

At first, when only a few hundred feet up, we could just discern the dusk shrouded roof tops of Downham Market, then quite quickly the familiar sight of the town disappeared into an opaque nothingness

Chapter 10 - Munich

becoming a black inverted bowl devoid of movement and life. Now that we were off the deck I removed a glove and cocked the guns with a round of ammunition in each, then put all the guns on "Fire". It would be an hour or two before we should normally be exposed to combat with an enemy aircraft, but there was always the possibility of the odd intruder aircraft appearing over the airfields or on the route out of England. The rule therefore was once airborne, all guns ready to fire. Below, the outer circuit of the airfield lights twinkled like a diamond necklace. Slowly we climbed and the sky gradually became lighter. On the ground it had been almost dark, but we were now out of the thin cloud and haze, and fast catching up with the watery sun until once again we saw the last of the sunset. The clouds had become quite thin over base, and we were treated once again to nature's masterpiece. It was incredibly beautiful and remote up here, with no artificial light, smoke or haze to detract from its beauty.

I never tired of this magnificent sight and it impressed me beyond words each time that I saw it. Above there were thin wispy clouds, whilst away in the distance a suggestion of mountainous cu-nim formations. Below lay velvet blackness, whilst at our level and above commenced a riot of colour; yellow, pink, orange, deep red, pale blue, aquamarine, mauve and then as one looked higher into the sky dark blue and finally a blackness in which the early stars glittered and twinkled. The whole maze of colours blended with and into the clouds making one incredible combination of hues and shades almost beyond description. For the first thirty minutes or so that we were flying we were going almost into the sunset, and all this time I gazed out contentedly and peacefully from the side of the turret at this constantly changing scene, altering continuously all the time yet always on the verge of beggaring description, until slowly it faded, becoming eventually a deep crimson glow which lingered and slowly merged into the darkness below.

My reverie was interrupted by the intercom bringing me back to harsher realities - "Oxygen on everybody". We had now reached 10,000ft and were settled on our course. Reaching down I felt for the Oxygen tube and finding it, connected it to my mask. Then individually, we each in turn spoke to the Skipper confirming "Oxygen on", after which all was quiet once more. At a height of 10,000ft it was mandatory to switch on oxygen. In point of fact we could have managed without it for a few thousand feet more, but better to err on the side of caution. It was known that this early imbibing of oxygen helped to keep one warm and psychologically it was an advantage. Depending upon the individual, but usually commencing at about 14,000 feet, lack of oxygen caused mental disorientation that became steadily worse as the height increased. It was a fact also that a victim of oxygen starvation was not conscious of his erratic behaviour and deterioration of mental processes. These were readily recognizable by an onlooker who was not deprived of oxygen.

We now altered course and against the darkness behind us I could see dozens of navigation lights gleaming on the aircraft that were following us. Soon they would be increased by hundreds of others as we and the main stream joined forces. This decorative and cheery sight would multiply, continuing until we reached the English coast when all lights would be turned off.

Red called me on the intercom to say that he had seen another Lanc fairly close on our port beam, but had lost sight of it as it moved across could I see it? Looking around I caught a glimpse of it, coming round our fin and rudder on the port quarter. It was about 200 yards away. This was quite close enough and I spoke to Emmie and warned him of its close proximity. For as long as we had our Nav lights on it was tolerably easy to see other aircraft around us. Both Red and I shared the searching of the skies when operating. We had a method of dividing the task up, each concentrating on our own portion of the sky in particular, although as far as was possible we endeavoured to watch everywhere. From Red's position in the mid-upper turret he could watch an aircraft from the front moving along either beam. The Pilot and Engineer could also see this portion of the sky. If the aircraft dropped or passed behind us, it then passed out of the mid upper's view into a blind spot behind the fin and rudder. At this stage, via the intercom, Red would pass it on to me and I would watch out until such time as it came into my sight. Similarly if I were watching an aircraft behind me or below, as soon as it commenced to move up onto the beam where I was going to lose it, I passed it on to Red. This constant watch was kept on all the aircraft visible to us, irrespective of whether they be friendly or possibly otherwise, thus lessening the risk of collision.

It was becoming cold now. Our height was around 18,000 feet and although breathing pure oxygen helped to keep us warm, it was insufficient on its own. For as long as possible I had left off the electric heating so as to gain maximum benefit when the cold began to seep through my clothing. The temperature was now 14 degrees below zero and rapidly becoming colder, so I turned on the heating switch. Quite quickly I felt

Chapter 10 - Munich

This view of the bomber mainstream was taken on the way to bomb the 'buzz' bomb sites in the Pas de Calais.

more comfortable and was able to give my full concentration once more to the task of watching other bombers. By now we were well in front of the main stream that stretched out behind us. As always on operations where we were used, the Pathfinder Force led the main force, and as deputy Master Bomber we were close to the head of the Pathfinders.

For a moment we caught the slipstream of another aircraft ahead of us. It bounced us about and we slewed to one side. Then Harry saw the Lanc ahead and the skipper manoeuvred Willie until once more we were flying straight and level. Soon after this we again caught up with another Lanc and had to repeat the action. On this occasion Harry caught sight of the aircraft's lettering - it was one of our own aircraft, G George, the first to take off from Downham Market. Our present position put us just about right in the order of things. There were only about six sets of Nav lights ahead of us, one of which would certainly be the Master Bomber, one of our own Squadron's aircraft.

The intercom hummed "Coast coming up" said Emmie - "About 15 miles ahead". We were dead on course and a contented sigh came from Ernie in the Nav's compartment. The coastline ahead had given him a perfect fix. Turning the turret onto the beam, and craning my neck, I

View from a Birdcage

Another view of the bomber mainstream.

could just discern the coast line at Beachy Head. Despite the darkness, it was always easy, even on the blackest night, to tell where the sea began. It appeared several shades darker than the land, not unlike comparing black against purple. Side by side one could see an unmistakable contrast. The configuration of the land also helps to separate land from water, and as had already happened, gives the Navigator a first class fix. Soon we should be away from England and not long afterwards, crossing the enemy coast. Mentally I checked everything once more but could think of nothing that had been forgotten. Feeling around the turret I found my ration bag and removed two sticks of gum to chew. Constantly breathing oxygen made the mouth feel very dry, and chewing gum was helpful. The remainder of the rations would be a welcome addition to our other rations and escape aids. We could never have too much food if, for instance, we were adrift in a dinghy. At times it was a big temptation, but apart from drinking the coffee - and then only after we had crossed the English coast on our return it was a self imposed rule that I had never broken.

Slowly now we crossed the coast below. Recognizable - by a headland which was Beachy Head - we could just make out the outline

Chapter 10 - Munich

of Eastbourne. A little to the other side of the town the beacon lights of a friendly airfield were flashing the Morse identification of the station. Emmie turned off the navigation lights. It was now very black outside, although the cu-nim was still well ahead of us. The stars above, by comparison, seemed brilliant. Ernie spoke on the intercom "We've gained three minutes on this leg skipper - I think we should do a dog leg over the sea and lose some of it". There was a short wait then Emmie turned the aircraft about 30 degrees to port, at the same time losing some height, and we commenced our time wasting leg. This turn was at a fairly sharp angle to the aircraft following, and we all kept a very keen outlook to port. In relation to ourselves, following aircraft would be coming up at a good clip on our beam heading towards us. Several did in fact come into our vision and whooshed by, just black shadows, a little darker than the night itself but with a faint glow showing from their exhaust systems. A little over a minute passed then we turned starboard and commenced returning to our original course. During the time that we had been out of the main stream we had requested permission from Emmie to fire our guns. This was normal operating procedure, and we fired our customary short bursts. This was barely more than a second or two, but as each Browning gun fired 1,200 rounds per minute, the fish below would receive a nasty shock! Once more a careful watch was kept whilst we were returning to the main stream, this time to starboard. We had now lost a little more than the two minutes required, and were back on course with sufficient time in hand to allow for what we hoped would be normal variations in wind and weather.

Ahead of us the enemy coast was coming up fast. On came the first searchlight and the flak, flickering orange and white flashes in the sky. Their height was accurate, just at our level, but a long way over to port, well clear of us. Well below we could see the curling trail of the light flak, a varied coloured stream with red, white, green and orange colours predominating. From above this light flak barrage appeared to move lazily in a slow curling arc, gradually falling away into the sea.

By now we were crossing the enemy coast, and below a new battery of searchlights came into being, illuminating the sky ahead and behind us. Momentarily we were bathed in a brilliant light and then it was gone. Mentally I cursed the lights. They had caught us unexpectedly, as a result I had no time at all to close one eye and thus preserve some night vision. At the moment I could see reasonably well, the close proximity to the searchlight battery making that possible, but as soon as they were extinguished my eyesight would have to commence recovery procedure. Alas for my hopes, Willie was suddenly caught and held by a master beam and in a moment or so dozens of additional lights moved over on to us. We were held in a brilliant cone. Emmie commenced evasive action to get out of the lights. Luckily the main belt of flak had been passed and we were bothered only by a desultory burst or two of inaccurate fire. The searchlights held on to us for a few minutes longer and we kept a sharp lookout for any new night fighters that might have seen us in the cone of light. Happily, all we could see were 20 or so other Lancasters in close proximity. Suddenly the lights went out and we enjoyed welcome obscurity.

The coastal defences were now rapidly receding and we were some 20 miles inside France and had reached our normal operational height of 20,000 feet. It was very cold and becoming increasingly so. The sky that had been about 4/10ths cloud covered was now building up to 10/10ths ahead of us, and really solid as far as we could see. Out to starboard the darkness ended with the arrival of fighter flares. Three of them came into being, destroying the comparative peace of our flight. They were not close enough to cause much alarm nor near enough to affect our night vision. Because of these flares, indicative of night fighter action, Emmie commenced a gentle weave banking left and right. This gave us a good opportunity to see below the aircraft, the favourite and most vulnerable spot for the Hun to commence his attack. If he were able to find a bomber just stooging along serenely and on a steady course, he would come creeping upwards from below and astern, and the first warning that the gunners would get was likely to be the fuselage being filled with bursting cannon shells and machine gun bullets.

Another trail of flares dropped astern of us, this time a little closer, and I had the comforting thought of the 10/10ths cloud ahead. This cloud must be fairly close now, and the idea of being enveloped in it did not seem nearly as objectionable as it had a short while ago. True it would mean heavy icing, if the Met forecast was correct, but there would be negligible risk of us being shadowed by Messchersmitts, Focke Wulfs and JU88s.

Astern there was a sudden glare in the sky - someone had hit something! First a string of traces fired from an invisible aircraft - then from its victim, a long sheet of flame, flickering a little and then suddenly becoming brighter. Whatever it was, it was going down fast. Then the flames reached the fuel and the whole machine became a flaming mass

Chapter 10 - Munich

of orange and red, diving down faster and faster, shedding masses of sparks and burning molten embers. The brilliance dimmed suddenly as it entered the last thin layer of cloud above the ground. For a few seconds it was relatively dark before hitting the earth, then came a terrific flare up in the final crash. For long seconds it lit the sky around us and I could see other aircraft in the reflected light, thankfully none of German origin. The illumination quickly faded until all that could be seen through the thin cloud below was a dull glowing mass, flickering for a short while and then dying away. Emmie reported the approximate position of the combat and Ernie noted this in his log. This information, in conjunction with that of other crews in the vicinity, would help to confirm either a fighter, or one of our bombers, shot down. The combat had been several miles away from us and too far to have been able to distinguish individual aircraft. Possibly some of our other aircraft would have been a lot closer and positive identification might have been made. I sincerely hoped that it had been a fighter.

We were flying steadily, and into cloud. Thin and wispy at first, but rapidly becoming thicker. It was comprised of huge grey woolly masses. Thankfully we were not yet accumulating ice. Minute globules of moisture were forming on the Perspex above my head and blowing continuously into the slipstream. They were soon likely to freeze, making a thin opaque covering of ice above my head. Vision directly above would then be impossible, but amidships Red could watch that area for me.

Willie was bumping along a lot now as we got deeper into the cloud. Not as a result of the slipstream from other aircraft but due to the turbulence inherent in a cumulus nimbus cloud formation. On the ends of my four gun barrels, St Elmo's fire (static electricity) had formed a blue halo, and was trickling across from one gun barrel to the other. It was quite harmless stuff and alarming only for the first time that it was experienced. Thereafter one became used to this phenomenon. Red was moaning about the ice which was forming rapidly on his turret, more so than on mine. He was facing astern most of the time and the panels behind his head were already thick with layers of frozen moisture. I looked out either side of my turret and could see the ends of our two radio aerials encrusted with ice and sagging with the additional weight. Emmie was making every effort to find a clear layer in which to fly. This hopefully would rid us of the ice, or at least prevent any more from forming. However, we were in some very solid stuff and there didn't seem to be much hope of getting into the clear at that time. The first malfunction occurred - the air speed indicator went u/s. Its pitot head (the fitting which directed the pressurised air into the indicator) was set in the leading edge of the fuselage and was electrically heated to prevent icing up. Apparently this heater was unserviceable or was unable to cope with the speed with which the ice was forming.

All the time Ernie and Frank were working together, plotting and obtaining fixes. I assumed that all was going well in the Navigation department for we had heard no moans from them over the intercom. Our last fix had put us over a town about 100 miles inside France and we should soon be altering course. Poor old Nobby must have been suffering terribly from all the interference and static which was a by product of the cu-nim cloud. He had to listen out continuously for any messages that might be transmitted from base. For a moment he switched his wireless receiver through the intercom circuit. The noise that came through the earphones was incredible. How he ever received an intelligible message, although it was in Morse, was beyond our comprehension. One of the required chores by the Wireless Operator was to broadcast back to base, by Morse, giving the direction and speed of the wind being encountered on the trip. The Nav team were able to supply this information for his transmission. More often than not, the forecast winds given to the crews at briefing were incorrect. On some occasions the forecast and actual winds differed greatly. With the revised information that was broadcast back to base, an amended wind forecast was radioed from Groups back to their aircraft. This updated information was invaluable, and could make a big difference to the success of the operation and the planned time on the target.

A faint smudge against the gloom on our port side fetched me back to life in a hurry. "Aircraft on port side up, Skipper, better to ease over to starboard". Emmie reacted immediately and altered course slightly, and dropped a couple of hundred feet. The smudge vanished and did not return. Once more we seemed to be on our own. It was unlikely that this had been a fighter, but almost certainly one of our own aircraft; however, chances were never taken. This one brief alteration of course and height had given us a bonus, since by making the alterations we had come out of the cloud bank into a reasonably clear lane between two layers of cloud. How long it would last was impossible to forecast, but we were not now building up ice, in fact we were losing a little of that which had already accumulated. My top panel cleared itself and shortly afterwards the air speed indicator began to function once more.

Suddenly I was tortured by the thought of that nice hot flask of coffee within arm's length. We had a long way to go as yet, and I tried to encourage less tantalising thoughts. I checked the gun heaters that I had switched on at 14,000 feet. They were all functioning and none of the breech blocks had frozen up. I had to take off my two outer pairs of gloves in order to test the heaters and the cold numbed my hands in a matter of seconds. "What's the temperature, Harry"? I asked. Harry replied "Minus 37". It seemed to be growing colder all the time, and so far this was one of the coldest trips with which we had had to contend so early in the trip. I had very quickly replaced my gloves, and sat on my hands for a short while until they became bearable. Ernie gave the Skipper an alteration in course, and we were heading now directly for the German border which was south east of our present position. By this time the German based radar would be picking up the approach of our force and would have an approximate idea of where we would cross the frontier. At about this time we, and all the other aircraft, would commence throwing out "window" – thin metallic strips which made detection by radar much more difficult. Harry usually did this job, despatching the strips through the flare chute situated close to the mid upper turret or occasionally from the Bomb Aimer's position in the nose. Many other tricks of the trade were involved in trying to keep secret our ultimate destination right up to the last possible moment. Of course there was no certainty in any of the trickery we adopted. We could hope for no more than adding to the difficulties of the German defences in deciding precisely which target we were going to attack. It was obviously completely impossible to make a very large force of bombers non-existent en route over hundreds of miles of German and German occupied territory. Night fighters, air defences and airborne interception all made certain that somewhere along the route we were going to be found and would be involved in combat. Generally the result of all the meticulous RAF planning worked out pretty well, though there were one or two notorious exceptions - Nuremburg for instance.

Our clear lane ended and once more we plunged into deep cloud. This time it was exceptionally bumpy. Even my vacuum flask jumped up and down, landing in my lap after one sudden dive. The very confined space in my turret at least kept me reasonably secure, and on occasions such as these I had reason to be pleased with my tight fit in the tail position. Dressed as I was, with the door shut, my head had about an inch clearance from the roof. My legs fitted tightly with the gun and turret control column between my legs, whilst my arms just touched the internal bracing of the turret on either side of me. A semi hunched up position had to be endured, and on an eight hour trip like this there were times when it became almost unbearable. When all normal means of dealing with cramp had failed, if conditions allowed – and this would only be when flying over England – I used to lock the turret centrally, open the doors and lay back, half in the turret, and the other half on the catwalk in the main fuselage. This gave a marvellous sensation and very quickly got rid of the cramps, though it was a very draughty business with the slip stream whipping in and around the turret and tail. Only on the rarest of occasions was I able to do this over enemy territory, and only when on daylight operations and with the Skipper's permission. On such occasions, since the tail position was blind, the mid upper gunner and the rest of the crew would keep a very sharp look out whilst I was thus engaged. Normally I left this relaxation until we had crossed the English coast on our return, to be followed by that longed for cup of coffee.

Briefly my thoughts wandered back to the days when we all came together at Rufforth and became a bomber crew. As nearly always happens, we came from totally different occupations. Emmie was in the family business of importing and exporting; Ernie was in banking in New Zealand; Frank in the family business of farming, mostly breeding and raising sheep – also in New Zealand; Nobby was a traveller in the stationery trade; Harry was a typewriter mechanic whilst Red was a peace time member of the Royal Air Force. Finally, I was an employee of a building society – quite a mixed bag!

My thoughts returned to the present. The cold was even more intense, and the air outlet of my oxygen mask was repeatedly gathering long icicles which had to be broken off. At one period I let it accumulate too much, and before I realised what was happening, I had a spike 10 or 12 inches long protruding from my mask. I must have looked like some creature from Greek mythology! Even more diabolical was the fact that my eyelashes began freezing together. I had to lift my goggles and put the palms of the heated gloves over my eyes to thaw the lids out. Usually one could avoid having this happen by blinking the eyes more than usual. On this occasion this exercise had been forgotten with the aforementioned result.

The air speed indicator was again frozen up and we were once more gathering a lot of ice. Even up in front, in the driver's compartment, they were beginning to feel the cold and I heard the Skipper asking Nobby to turn up the heat. The front of the fuselage, being all enclosed was infinitely warmer than it was at the rear end since it was receiving hot air along the ducts running direct from one of the engines. Even so, they were now finding the cold penetrating in spite of this heating.

The Navigation team now had a moan going. The forecast wind directions and velocity had gone haywire. It seemed to be blowing from every direction, never remaining constant for more than a few minutes at a time. Frank got another fix (it must have been a fluke – obtained on Gee at extreme range). This put us more or less on course, but we had gained about 11 minutes, and therefore had about 14 minutes in hand. Ernie had a discussion with Emmie as to the advisability of losing some of his excess time by doing another time–wasting leg. It was decided to defer this for a while. With the winds as erratic as they now were, there was always the possibility that we would find that there was a headwind to contend with instead of the beam wind that had been predicted that in the main had been correct, though the estimated wind speeds were way out.

If in fact we were to encounter a strong head wind, we could very easily lose some if not all of the surplus time in hand. Additionally, dog legs in thunder clouds were potentially hazardous since the possibility of collision with other aircraft in the vicinity was ever present. The thought of turning more or less at right angles to the main stream containing hundreds of Lancasters and Halifaxes did not bear thinking about. It was finally decided that if we had all this time to spare we would then, when reasonably near to the target, do our dog leg over German territory, particularly as the Met forecast suggested the likelihood of cloud clearance in the vicinity of the target.

The cloud continued to get thicker and thicker, and the temperatures even lower. It was now 42 degrees below zero. I wished very hard for a clear patch of cloud in which to fly, fighters or no fighters. This blanked out feeling became very tiring, continually looking out, port, starboard, port, starboard, up, down, up, down trying to see something which you know will never be seen until it is dangerously close, always assuming that you did eventually see it! By now we had collected a dangerous amount of ice, with Willie consequently very sluggish in responding to the controls. Finding a bit of cloud free sky was about our only chance of getting rid of this excess weight.

Unaccountably the air speed indicator began to function normally. This was a great relief to the Pilot and Navigator. When it was unserviceable, the speed had to be judged by the engine rev counters, and by the feel of the engines and aircraft. Emmie had been making a pretty good job of it, but nonetheless, was happy when it was no longer a matter of judgement. In addition this would mean that the temperature was rising though as yet I had no sense of this happening. I began to feel the first twinges of cramp and moved by body about as best I could. An inch or two in any direction was all that I could manage, but auto suggestion was at work and I really felt that I had made myself more comfortable. Possibly this was so, but if it was it didn't last for more than a few minutes. I commenced to sing out loud anything that came to mind. This was my habit when I was cheesed off and in extreme discomfort. It always seemed to be a good way of letting off steam, particularly since there was nothing else that I could do. Even when I screamed my head off, nothing could be heard, not even by me. Of course I could turn on the intercom and serenade the whole of the crew, earning myself a lot of doubtful compliments.

Red called me and asked if I could see anything slightly below on the starboard quarter. I strained my eyes but not a thing showed through the grey murk around us, although it did seem to me that the cloud wasn't quite so dense. Hearing Red's voice had keyed me up and made me forget my own discomfort. I commenced to take a very keen interest in this area, watching where he believed that he had seen a light. If there was one it should show up again. I thought also of the possibility of another aircraft nearby, perhaps its exhaust systems glowing. All this sudden interest made me oblivious of my recent attack of cramp.

Flying continuously in cloud is an insidious business. Almost unconsciously one can become lax in searching the skies, or rather trying to pierce the cloud, being lulled into an easy but false sense of security by the dense blanket of mist around the aircraft. Again Red spoke saying that he was sure that he had seen a light, still in roughly the same area. Again I searched diligently, noting that the cloud was undoubtedly thinning. Eventually I sensed the ground below and saw a small light twinkling far below on the starboard quarter. We were too high to be certain of the source of the light, but I felt that there was a rhythm in the flashing, deciding eventually that it could be a powerful torch or signalling lamp. Within the last minute or two the cloud had almost cleared from below and the light was still pointing in our general direction. Then I recognised that the rhythm of the flashes was Morse. I watched intently- dit, dit, dit, dah- dit, dit, dit, dah- V, V for Victory! It must have been a French

Chapter 10 - Munich

civilian, or possibly a member of the Underground giving us a welcome as we went overhead. To us it was a cheery, heartening sight, one that we had seen on several occasions when over occupied territory. There was quite a temptation, for I felt that I should reply to this friendly message, with an answering sign of "Good Luck" from our aircraft.

Wondering exactly what our position was, I called up Ernie and asked where we were. His reply was "Half an hour from the German frontier if we keep going as we are now. Better keep your eyes skinned for we are near enough for the home based fighters to be around". Although we were now in the clear, a little above us stretched an apparently unbroken cloud base. Emmie climbed a few hundred feet and we were now near enough to make a quick exit in the cloud should any fighters materialise. Being so close to the cloud base was a great help in our search since we could disregard what was above, other than an occasional quick look, thus concentrating at our own level and below. On the port side, a long way to the east, there was a faint glow of searchlights. I asked Ernie what they might be. He replied "Probably Karlsruhe". It was apparent that they knew that we were in the vicinity and were taking no chances.

We were now rapidly unfreezing. All the ice had gone from the Perspex on the turrets, and I could see that the radio aerials were gradually assuming their normal dimensions. As we still had plenty of time in hand it was decided to lose a few minutes while we were out of the cloud. Accordingly, with all eyes on the lookout, we turned off to port, across the main stream. We were in good company for we caught sight of a number of blurs as other Lancs and Hallis passed us forging steadily ahead. Presumably they would do their dog legs later on; otherwise they were going to be very early on the target! By now we were well away from the main stream, and after two further minutes of flying Ernie asked the Skipper to turn back starboard and re-join the other aircraft, on our original course. We had lost a 1,000ft to minimise the risk of collision, and we made our way back to the middle of the stream, regaining height more slowly. One more alteration on to course and we were all set, with two minutes in hand for emergencies.

The intercom hummed; "Crossing the German frontier" said Frank. Everything seemed to be the same and as yet no activity other than the same glow of searchlights in the distance. Soon we were routed well clear of this city, but there always seemed to be the odd wanderer who got a little too close for comfort. I felt very content with our Nav team, for despite very adverse conditions, they had never made that kind of error.

Underneath us there would now be mountainous country – not nice for emergency or crash landings, and with very hostile residents on the look out for such happenings. All the time that we had been over occupied France there was always a good chance that if such an emergency arose, we should have received care and sustenance from the Underground. Thousands of members of aircrews had received such help and owed their lives and freedom to the magnificent help that these patriots had afforded them. There would be no such assistance for us in the area below. We'd become evaders in the worst possible country and weather, with only an outside chance of reaching the French border, and this chance was lessening with each further minute of flying time.

The Stuttgart searchlight came on. They were ahead and on our port side, as yet we could see no flak. I began to feel a bit twitchy. This apparent lack of any enemy hostility, excluding the searchlights, didn't seem to be normal. I could feel my eyes sticking out on stalks as I searched intently. I was determined that we shouldn't be surprised by a fighter if I could possibly help it. Red called up to enquire if everything was all right, and whether I had seen anything like trouble. I reassured him – apparently I wasn't the only member of the crew who felt keyed up. Nobby, Ernie and Frank were all enclosed behind curtains in their respective positions and couldn't see a thing outside. It must have been a lot worse for them, for at least we could see if anything happened or was likely to happen.

They all knew that there was a possibility of meeting hostiles at any time, and relied on Red, Harry, Ernie and myself watching and keeping out of trouble. Again I thought of the cloud and unpleasant though it was, it had at least been a good hiding place in an emergency. By now the cloud had cleared entirely leaving a clear starlit sky above. Fortunately for us the moon would be very late in rising, and if all went well we should be home, and perhaps in bed, before it came up. The gum which I had been chewing ever since leaving England had lost all its flavour. I put some more in my mouth and carried on with the search.

Action suddenly commenced. Over to starboard, just a few hundred yards away, a string of tracer bullets curved through the air. The approximate position of the aircraft that was firing them could be judged, although we were unable to see it as yet. There was no answering fire from its target. We edged away slightly to be at a safe distance and I continued to watch intently while Red searched the opposite side of the sky in case trouble developed from that quarter. Very often, two fighters would work

Chapter 10 - Munich

as a team. One would appear on one side of the bomber, deliberately firing a burst out of range to draw the bomber crew's attention, whilst the other fighter would come in close from the opposite side hoping that the gunners, attention had been drawn away from him. He would then open fire on the bomber, very often at point blank range.

The firing ceased with no apparent results. A few seconds passed, then the firing commenced again, this time both aircraft firing at each other. Results came quickly. A sheet of orange flame, and the outline of one of the combatants could be seen. It was a twin engined fighter, an ME110 and it was on its back and going down fast. Suddenly the cockpit canopy flew off, and one member of the aircraft catapulted out, turning over and over. He was quickly gone from sight and I didn't see his parachute open, though there was still plenty of time. The other member of the crew had been trapped in the fighter, possibly killed or injured in the attack, and did not get out of the machine which was now a blazing torch. Eventually we saw the fighter explode on the ground, a brilliant flash then hundreds of pieces of glowing embers scattering over a wide area. I opened the one eye that I had closed to preserve night vision since the combat had commenced and carried on the search as before. Although the attack had been uncomfortably close, the tension had been relieved and I felt considerably better. It was also a terrific boost to my morale that the bombers gunners had been wide awake, efficiently despatching their attacker. All being well that crew would be celebrating upon their return to base.

We were now quite close to Stuttgart, and sure enough the flak started to come up. Then the inevitable straggler appeared. A searchlight picked him up and immediately about twenty other lights moved over and held him in a cone of brilliance. Up came the flak, seemingly along the searchlight beams, bursting all around him in vicious orange and black spurts. I felt sorry for the crew; they were having a pretty horrifying experience. It was too far away to be able to tell exactly how close the shells were bursting but obviously it was too close to be healthy. Suddenly, for no apparent reason, all the lights went out. The flak ceased immediately afterwards, and a very lucky aircraft and crew found themselves at peace again and still flying on. The sudden cessation of lights and flak was puzzling, yet we had seen it happen on other occasions with a bomber held in the cone: it didn't make sense. We were doing a very good weave now, with a decided banking motion, as a result of which we were able to keep a good watch below against surprise attack.

Maintaining a good firm grip on the turret controls and triggers, I swung the turret steadily, full to port, back round, full to starboard and then back once again, continuing the search all the time. It took about 10 seconds for a full sweep and searching every inch of the sky that I could see. I knew that Red would be keeping an equally intense look out, concentrating particularly on that part of the sky that I was unable to cover. Emmie and Harry too, would be concentrating to the front in the direction of travel, and Nobby had taken over in the astro dome, a small bubble of Perspex on top of the fuselage. He also occupied this position when we were running up over the target.

Fighter flares went down ahead of us and to starboard. Two rows of six flares each, forming a lane through which the fighters hoped that we might fly. The flares were a couple of miles off our course and Emmie pressed on. We had friendly company with us. In the faint light cast by the flares I could see two Lancs, one on either side of us, both of which were also weaving in unison with ourselves. Luckily we were each at slightly different levels as we crossed and re-crossed each other during our weaving. We should be less likely to have an attack while we were in a bunch, since stragglers were preferred by fighters whenever possible.

It was so cold now that all my clothing, plus the electric heating, couldn't keep me really warm. Upon enquiring, Harry said that the temperature had dropped to 51 degrees below zero. This was the second coldest trip that we had so far experienced. My eyelashes were threatening to freeze together again and only continuous blinking kept them free. Even so, they had a peculiar gummy feeling as I blinked them free. Fortunately my hands and feet were reasonably warm, but I wouldn't care to take the risk of removing my gloves during the present conditions. Earlier, when first getting into thinner cloud, we had lost the bulk of the excess ice on Willie. The ice that remained was not excessive and would not build up again now that we were in comparatively moisture free air.

We made our last alteration but one, turning slightly to the north. In view of the fact that all of our aircraft were steadily converging, we knew that we were in close company with our fellow travellers. It was an anxious moment though all went well. Once more, having left the fighter flares well astern, it was very dark. We could no longer see our two companions though I sensed that they were near. We roared steadily onwards. Stuttgart lay well astern now and probably, with the exception of the fighters, there would be no further trouble until we were in the vicinity of the target when flak could once more be expected.

Chapter 10 - Munich

Our timing was now working out quite well and we had just three minutes in hand. The winds had settled down, resulting in a contented Nav team. Also, for better or worse, it looked as though the remainder of our trip was to be done under cloud free conditions. A smudge whipped by overhead and I gripped the triggers tightly, and pressed the intercom switch ready to give immediate evasive action if required. Just in time I made out the four faint glows from engine exhausts. Another Lanc no doubt, and I relaxed once more. I heard the intercom, then Red's voice "Did you see that aircraft Jack, it just went over to starboard?" I answered – "Ok Red, I saw it, it was another Lanc. I'll concentrate on starboard, you watch port".

Our weaving was now more violent, not sufficient to take us off course, but quite enough to give us good downward visibility. The ground below was now covered by snow and it was possible to pick out some good ground details. Woods, lakes and rivers showed up particularly well as dark patches and black winding lines. These conditions also meant that we should make a very nice silhouette for any fighters above us, so we both spared a little extra time searching in that area. Frank obtained a fix for Ernie. We were still on course, with very mountainous country below. A long way to starboard we could see a faint but extensive glow, the lights of a town in war – free Switzerland. On our way home we should be much closer to the Swiss frontier, and I looked forward to getting a much better view of this long forgotten phenomenon. A clutch of flares dropped right below us, about 2,000 feet down. This wasn't good – there would be fighters somewhere nearby, approximately at our level or perhaps above us. We would make a lovely picture from above and Red concentrated entirely up there while I kept an eye below and at our level. Harry reported a combat going on ahead of us, but a little later it terminated and once more all was quiet.

Events were certainly beginning to liven up and I felt a bit hot under the collar, even though we were leaving the fighter flares behind. This affected me physically to the extent that I turned off the heating for a couple of minutes. Very soon the extreme physical discomfort overcame my fear and I turned the heat on again. My throat was parched and I popped some more gum into my mouth and indulged in some steady chewing. The target couldn't be far off, about 50 minutes I guessed. I looked forward to getting there, and getting the hell out of Germany! The flares had receded into the distance and could no longer be seen. No other Lancs were visible but I hoped that some were nearby. All of a sudden, quite close to our port quarter, a navigation light showed. It was at a reasonable distance from us, but at our height and travelling at the same speed. I warned Red to keep a good watch to starboard while I continued to watch the light to port. Nobby took time of from his radio and shared the search with us while Harry watched out ahead.

We hadn't much doubt what it was all about; it was the Hun with one of his favourite tricks. Again they worked in pairs on this slightly altered variation to trap the bomber. When a bomber had been sighted, one fighter would go out of range of the bomber's guns, then switch on his navigation lights drawing the attention of the bomber crew. As explained, we had already had the earlier variation demonstrated. If the gunners fell victim to this trick, the other fighter would waste no time in diving in with guns and cannons blazing, making what he hoped would be an unopposed attack with fatal results to any unwary victim. Luckily, this and other similar decoy systems were becoming widely known, and thus met with little or no success.

We continued watching, but nothing developed and eventually we relaxed. If they had been working a bomber, it hadn't been us; the nav lights gradually faded away into the distance, finally vanishing. It seemed unnaturally quiet now no flares, fighters, flak or searchlights. This should have been a relief, but somehow I couldn't imagine that the rest of the trip to the target was going to be free of trouble. It seemed as if we were alone. I hadn't seen another Lanc for some time; neither did I sense the presence of any in our vicinity.

It must, by now, have been time for another RAF raid to commence – this one on Nuremburg. When attending our briefing we had noted that this other target was to be hit that night, and for this reason were on the look out for this attack to commence. It was due to commence some time before our attack started. Altogether on the Briefing Room list, there were six other attacks besides our own, one other being a fairly large attack on Nuremburg, and five lesser attacks, two of them being nuisance raids. These nuisance raids were usually carried out by our very good friends in the Mosquitos. They would normally go out in pairs, unarmed but flying very fast and high. Their purpose was to cause the maximum alarm and despondency to town dwellers and night workers below. For its size, the "Mossie" could carry quite a hefty bomb load – around 4,000 lbs. Result – all of the inhabitants were out of their beds, and even more importantly, away from their factories, just as though it had been a major raid. In addition, a certain proportion of German night fighters were involved in

Chapter 10 - Munich

what were minor raids, thus to some extent lessening the strain on the major bomber streams taking part in heavier raids on the same night. The Mosquitos relied for their protection on their great speed and very high operating ceiling.

Our other good friends were the boys from 100 Group. They flew a fair number of four engined aircraft, but didn't usually carry a bomb load since they were loaded down with radio countermeasures and all the latest "gen" boxes that were being constantly updated. Their usual route was to stooge up and down the North Sea while we were operating on German towns and cities, though on some occasions they flew with us in the bomber stream. More often than not, the equipment that was carried played havoc with the German radio and radar, and must undoubtedly have been the means of saving many a British bomber from an early demise. Some of this Group's aircraft were B17s – Flying Fortresses supplied by the US on Lend Lease. Many of the aircraft carried an additional member of the crew who spoke fluent German. These crew members broadcast counter instructions to the German night fighters. They used the same frequency as the enemy transmitters and caused a lot of havoc among the fighter pilots. They were very unpopular with the enemy.

Despite all the assistance from the aforementioned sources, we were to learn later at debrief that tonight's raids had suffered many casualties from fighters and flak – proof that at this period of the war the Luftwaffe, extended though it was, was still able to put up a massive armada of night fighters into the sky, mostly ME110s and JU88s with a smaller number of ME109s and FW190s. Fortunately for us, at this stage the rocket and jet aircraft had not yet put in an appearance.

Nobby came onto the intercom; "Listen to this chaps". He then switched the radio over onto the intercom circuit. He'd picked up a broadcast from a German night fighter control unit. We knew little German but because of what was being broadcast, it was reasonably intelligible. They were broadcasting strings of figures to the already airborne night fighters, vectoring them onto the main bomber stream. It was not possible for us to decipher to which stream the fighters were being directed because of the two raids in this area, maybe one or other of the attacks, or maybe all of us. Anyway, it didn't make pleasant listening, hearing them reeling off these figures, and sounding very confident in the process.

Emmie asked Nobby to commence a "Mandrel" broadcast. Mandrel was the code name of a very useful British countermeasure against

103

View from a Birdcage

German fighter control broadcasts such as that which we had just listened to. In one of the engine bays there was a microphone wired directly to Willie's radio transmitter. Once the German broadcast frequency was found, the Wireless Operator set his transmitter up onto the same waveband, threw a switch that connected the microphone and broadcast to the fighters the deafening noise of a Rolls Royce engine at high revs. This cacophony of sound suddenly invaded the German fighters' cockpit causing unbelievable havoc. It was later learned that the German radio boffins largely overcame the problem which was plaguing their pilots, but not before very good results had been obtained by the Royal Air Force.

Quiet again descended on Willie. Everyone in the crew who could be spared was searching the skies intently, which in effect meant that only Ernie, navigating behind his curtains, was not so engaged. We forged steadily onwards. Red was the first to see the commencement of the attack on Nuremburg. It was away to the north, but the red and green markers dropped by the Pathfinders together with target indicators could easily be distinguished, far away as they were. Shortly afterwards the incendiaries began to shower down and the distant glow increased. It was too far away to be able to see what the opposition was like, but knowing the area it was probably intense.

Emmie decided to lose another minute of our time in hand. The two minutes that would remain could be lost by a slight decrease in speed. Accordingly we turned, did a quick dog leg and came back onto course. No other aircraft had been seen during these manoeuvres, but before commencing our turn we had climbed about 1,500ft. The other aircraft were probably a bit below us, somewhere between 18-20,000ft.

I checked the guns again for a possible freeze up, this time without removing my gloves. They were all OK and ready for instant use. Sometimes I had an overpowering desire to press these triggers just to make certain that they were in good order. There were however many reasons why this was undesirable, so I always resisted the temptation. In addition, because every gunner was responsible for the maintenance of his own guns and turret, he knew they were all right – or else!

There was another 30 minutes to go before running up onto the target and the final alteration of course could shortly be made. Over to port, some distance away, two green flares had dropped. We had been told about these at briefing. They were two dummy markers dropped by our own aircraft, probably Mosquitos, and were intended to confuse the German night fighters and other defences. I hoped that all the fighters in

Chapter 10 - Munich

this area were heading for these flares! They would find nothing there and it would give us valuable breathing space. The chaps who had the job of dropping these spoof markers had had a long, lonely trip and their efforts were very much appreciated by the main force of bombers. We had proof that they frequently achieved their purpose.

Alas, my hopes of peace and lack of fighters were in vain. Two combats commenced simultaneously, both to our port side. At this moment a dark blur shot across our stern, no more than 200 yards behind us, and close enough to identify the silhouette of an ME110. I almost fired, but in a split second, realised that the pilot hadn't seen us, and was making for one of the combats already taking place. In addition, any aircraft passing at a very high speed, and at right angles to us, was an almost impossible shot. To have even the faintest chance of hitting him, I would have needed to have seen him way out on the beam. I advised the Skipper of the near encounter and continued searching. The two combats on the port continued for a while, but were inconclusive and eventually died away. It was now dark again apart from the faint glow from the fast disappearing green flares.

Twenty minutes to go now, and Ernie gave the skipper a slight correction to our course and we edged slowly over to starboard. We had reduced height slightly and were down to about 19,000 feet. For a moment I caught a glimpse of another Lancaster close by. It was quite clear now; just cold bright starlight above, but far below a thin layer of cloud was building up to 10/10ths cloud cover. Again my mouth had become very dry and I freshened up the chewing gum with another stick which helped to moisten my mouth and throat.

Emmie and Harry were looking out intently ahead of us. Our attack was due to start with the first markers going down at minus twelve minutes from zero hour. Very soon we should cease weaving, and I would have to centralise and lock my turret ready for the bombing run. As yet we had heard nothing from the Master Bomber who would by now be circling the target above the rest of us. Hopefully he would be able to conduct his task without calling us in. The job of the Master Bomber was to be first on the target and drop the initial markers. He then climbed several thousand feet above the main force, circling the target area, assessing both his own markers and the result of the attack as it progressed. Even though the aiming point had been well marked by him, and by following members of the Pathfinder Force, there was a tendency as the raid progressed, for the bombing pattern to creep backwards from the initial aiming point. In the event of this happening the Master Bomber re-marked the aiming point correctly with a marker of a different colour to the original. Alternatively, he might call upon his deputy (us on this raid), or another Pathfinder aircraft to do so. Accuracy and continuing accuracy in the marking of the target usually meant a successful raid.

It will be seen that the Master Bomber's duty was vital to the success of the attack. As he remained over the target until conclusion of the raid, he was the first aircraft to arrive and the last to leave. After his initial bombing he overflew the target, circling around until all the bombing had been completed, being overhead for perhaps 20 minutes. Needless to say the Germans soon became aware of the importance of the Master Bomber and spared no effort to shoot him down once the raid had started and they knew that he was there.

It was not a very enviable job and was only given to the most experienced Pathfinder pilots. Strangely there was no shortage of volunteers, though the duty was allocated rather than offered. As deputy Master Bomber we were the back up on hand to take over from the Master if he had any problems or was shot down. In case of the former event the Master would call us up on the radio, instructing us to take over the task. In the latter event, we should know by the absence of the markers that he had failed to arrive and had presumably been shot down. We would then automatically take over the job, albeit a few minutes late. The only time that two British bombers over enemy territory communicated by plain language on the radio was in the calls mentioned above. All other communication between aircraft engaged on a raid, or over enemy territory, was conducted in Morse and usually only between the aircraft and its base.

Nobby was again listening out for any messages from the Master, and heard his first instructions which he relayed to the Skipper. All was well so far. "Minus 12 minutes" said Emmie, and almost simultaneously Harry said "Green and red markers going down to starboard – about 5 degrees correction, Emmie." We turned slightly and the bombing run commenced. The intercom hummed "Lock rear turret Jack." I replied, "OK Skipper, confirm turret locked." The moment had come – how I hated rendering myself immobile! I centralised and locked the turret. This was essential because when on the bombing run the slightest movement of the rear turret would throw the aircraft a degree or so off course, which greatly upset Frank who was now in the Bomb Aimer's position in the nose where he was endeavouring to steer Emmie correctly

Chapter 10 - Munich

to the aiming point.

I stretched up as far as was possible, and tried to peer out in all directions at the same time. I could hear Red talking to Harry who had seen the flak coming up ahead of us. It appeared to be pretty accurate, but not yet intense though it would soon increase. We were still too far away to be affected by it. The cloud below completely covered the ground although it was quite thin and the Master marker and the later markers could be clearly seen through the thin cloud. It would not be necessary to drop sky markers or use H_2S. Above us the sky remained clear. Flares were beginning to cascade down and the flak increased dramatically.

All the searchlight batteries were now operating but they were unable to pierce the cloud. Nonetheless, the diffused light made everything remarkably clear, and we could now see Lancasters and Halifaxes everywhere, some being very close to us.

Another few minutes to go before we were due to drop our markers and bomb. This was a long run up; sometimes we had only a few minutes on the bombing run. It all depended on the target and the aiming point. I could see four Lancasters, all within two hundred yards of us. It was very easy to see now, in the increasing glow from the fires below and the diffused light of the searchlights coming through the clouds. Because of this there was now no hope of retaining good night vision although it wasn't needed under the present conditions. Red reported that the flak was easing up which probably meant that the fighters were around and drawing in for a kill. As if to mock Red's words, there was a sudden burst of heavy flak just below and astern of us. I couldn't smell the burst although I could see that it had been very close, since the concussion of the explosion had shaken the aircraft and my turret in particular. Judging the distance from where the flak had burst was not always easy. If luck were not running with you, you could be hit by fragments from a shell burst that was quite a distance away. Conversely, a near miss might result in nil or negligible damage. The one thing that we quickly learned was that if a burst was really close the explosive fumes could be smelt. In my open ended turret I was usually the first one to have my nostrils assailed! Still we kept steadily on course. No weaving now, just a small prayer that things didn't get too bad – and searching the sky intently all the time but without the benefit of rotating the turret. It was heartening to see many other Lancs above us and behind, as well as keeping station on either side. I even managed to wave my hand at another gunner on the nearest aircraft and he duly returned the greetings. Hopefully we both felt a bit better for this exchange of good wishes. There was no attempt at formation flying despite our close proximity to each other. Each aircraft and crew were on their own with just one purpose in mind – striving to get spot on to the target, drop their bombs and then away from the scene as quickly as possible.

Four minutes to go now and it was becoming lighter by the minute. Fortunately the change back to blackout conditions on the run out of the target would be gradual, allowing plenty of time for the eyes to acclimatise and finally become fully night adapted. I looked now, mostly on the dark side of the sky, that being the most likely direction from which an attack would commence whilst we were near or over the target.

A myriad of Lancs and Hallis could now be seen all over the sky. They were dotted around at differing heights and directions, but all steadily converging on the aiming point ahead. I kept a very wary eye on one Lancaster almost directly overhead hoping that he would have moved over to one side before he opened his bomb-bay doors. I was sweating now, as I always did over the target; of such things is fear made! There were many, many occasions, particularly on the bombing run, when I asked myself why I had volunteered for this lousy job. It was on these occasions that I truly knew the meaning of fear, and I was never able to give myself a satisfactory answer to my self imposed question. Strangely enough, upon our return from any particularly hazardous trip such was the uplift in my spirits that I looked forward eagerly to the next operation. I was used by now to this sweating – certainly it must be caused by tension and fear, but I knew that it would be short lived. As usual, I switched off the electric heating. This would remain off until we had dropped our bombs and were on our way out of the target area.

Three minutes to go, and by now it was like subdued daylight. Harry had reported a very large explosion and one enormous fire in the target area, these being started by the first aircraft over the target. These fires and searchlights were responsible for the very light conditions in which we now found ourselves. Looking at the raging fires below, my mind went back to my earlier war time experiences, particularly in the winter of 1940, when as a fire fighter I had experienced all the major London air raids. I knew at first hand what the civil defence below were going through, as well as the civilian population. Sadly, pity was not one of my thoughts for I too had had to endure being at the top of a ladder whilst the German bombs were whistling down, and I had also seen comrades killed.

Chapter 10 - Munich

Below me a Halifax was smoking from its port outer engine. I had seen nothing to cause it but the next time that I looked the smoke had died away and all seemed normal. A stream of tracers down on the port side caught my eye. It was the first combat that I had seen over the target. I guessed it as being about a mile away, but as it was so light I could just make out that the bomber was being attacked by a single engined fighter, probably an ME109. Having completed the first attack without any success, the ME broke away and came in for another curve of pursuit attack. This time the bomber's gunners really got down to it. Two converging streams of tracer went out to meet that of the fighter. The Hun broke down and away. I thought that he might have had enough, then I saw a glow in the nose of his machine, then one big burst of flame and he was gone. Good for the gunners! One more Mess party would be taking place some hours ahead if all went well. I made a mental note of this combat, so that in due course I could pass it on to Ernie for a log entry.

Two minutes to go before releasing the bombs. I could hear Frank, from the Bomb Aimer's position, giving Emmie occasional corrections as we neared the target and aiming point. I was watching dead astern, plenty of bombers following us – then my scalp prickled! About 50 yards behind us was the perfect outline of an aircraft which I had learned to know intimately during my many training hours on aircraft recognition – a Junkers 88 twin engined night fighter. I immediately adjusted my ring sight to accommodate the wing span of the aircraft, then saw that it was going straight up, then turning to port, making a perfect plan form against the sky but too far away to have any chance of hitting it. Part of my mind was all tense and alert watching whether he was coming back to attack us, while the other part of my mind was reminding myself how like it was to the diagrams and photographs which we had seen so many times during our long hours at lectures. Down he eventually flew, out of sight, and I breathed freely once more.

During this time Red and Nobby had been watching with me, then Nobby took over the search with me while Red concentrated on the other side of the sky. All this had taken only about 30 seconds, not the life time that it had seemed. We settled down to the last minute of the bombing run – "Bomb doors open" said Frank. There was a sudden drag on the aircraft and it seemed, to pause momentarily, in the sky – "Bomb doors open" repeated Emmie, and Ernie commenced to count off the seconds to the release point. "Fifty seconds to go", we all kept quiet – no talking unless it was really vital. "Forty seconds to go". I looked up above to see the

Lanc that had worried me by his closeness. He was now just far enough behind us for his bombs to miss us. The bomb doors, like ours, were open and I could see his clusters of flares and markers plus 1,000 lb high explosive bombs set in the middle of the bomb bay, and one "Cookie", weighing 4,000 lbs.

"Thirty seconds to go". We were tightly surrounded now by dozens of Lancs and Hallis. Twenty, nineteen, eighteen, seventeen, sixteen seconds to go. I was wishing very hard now; let's drop these bombs and get the hell out of the danger zone. Six, five, four, three, two, one – "Now". Willie suddenly lifted and felt very buoyant. "Bombs gone Skipper", came Frank's voice. We continued flying straight and level waiting for the photo flash to drop, and for the camera to take automatically a series of photographs of the area that we had bombed. These photos, and all the others taken by every aircraft on the raid, would be interpreted by the Intelligence Sections on our return to base.

At last it was over. I heard Emmie's voice saying "Bomb doors closing – bomb doors closed". With a sigh of relief, I unlocked my turret and returned to the business of searching for fighters. I quickly became conscious of the cold and turned on the heating. Once again Willie was doing a lovely weave, and as a consequence I had an excellent view below. A cluster of bombs left a Lancaster about half a mile astern looking like a string of beads, and glittering as they caught the light of the fires below.

• • • • • •

Chapter 10 - Munich

"Bombs away"(1000 pounders). The campaign of strategic bombing carried out by Bomber Command and the USAF 8th Air Force materially affected the course of the Second World War in Europe. The pictures on the following pages show the wide range of targets identified, struck, damaged and destroyed during this campaign and are testimony to the vital role of Bomber Command.

View from a Birdcage

Hamm railway marshalling yard.

Bielefeld railway viaduct.

Chapter 10 - Munich

Destruction in Berlin in an area south of the Tiersgarten. An area approximately 1150 x 850 yards has been gutted by incendiary bombs.

View from a Birdcage

Hamburg burning 26/7/43.

Bombing of sea defences at Walcheren, Holland, prior to invasion.

Chapter 10 - Munich

A bomb battered German night fighter airfield on the north coast of France.

Ruins of an oil production plant at Bochum in the Ruhr.

View from a Birdcage

Heligoland - heavily battered.

A raid in progress on a Pas de Calais rocket launching site. 12,000 lb bombs were used. One Lancaster below is seen on its bombing run.

Chapter 10 - Munich

After the famous 'Dambusters' raid on the Moehne dam this aerial picture was taken 13 miles downstream. It shows submerged roads, isolated electricity works, destroyed road and railway bridges, wrecked railway coaches and submerged sidings.

View from a Birdcage

Before. The explosive works and depot at Salbris, 35 miles south west of Orleans in France, captured by RAF reconnaissance aircraft.

Chapter 10 - Munich

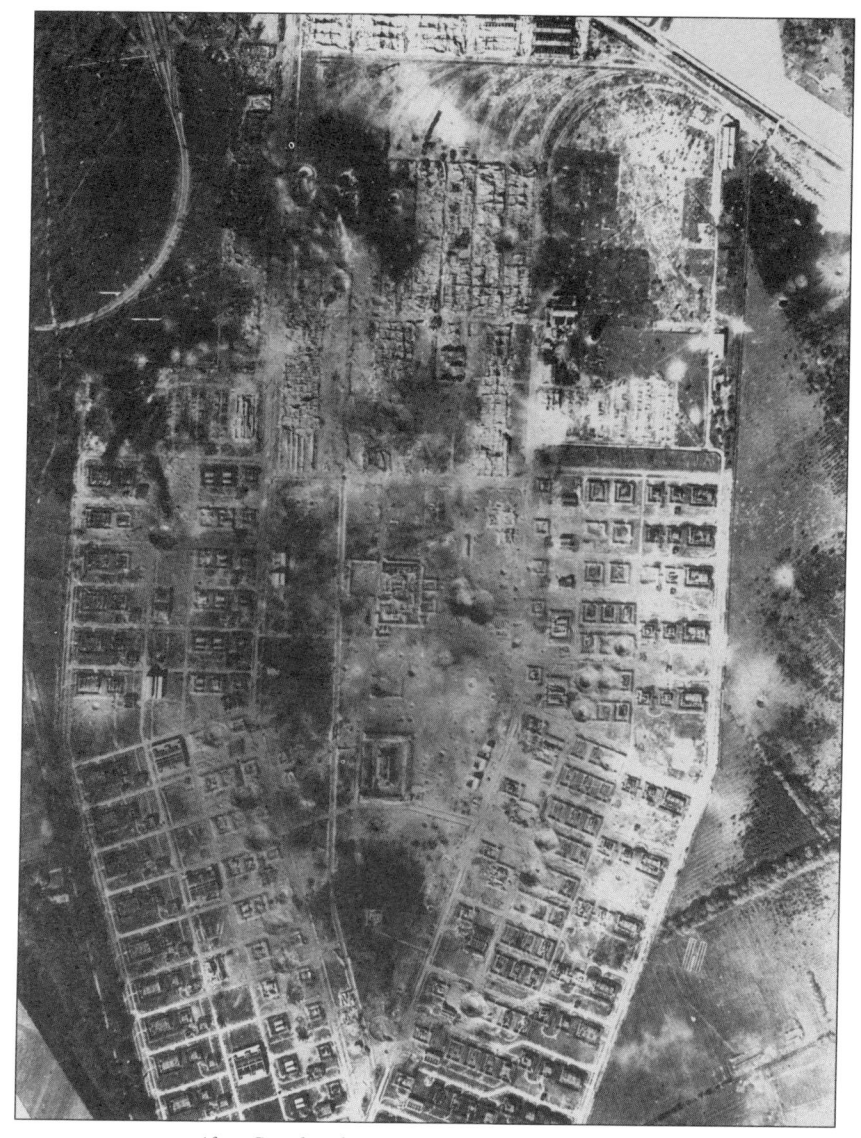

After. Complete destruction and devastation after a Bomber Command strike.

View from a Birdcage

A raid in progress on Cologne, 2nd March 1945. The Deutz road suspension bridge has collapsed and the superstructure of the Hohenzollern bridge has also collapsed. Note that the Cathedral is undamaged.

Chapter 10 - Munich

An attack by Mosquitoes on a German fighter airfield. An ME109 can be seen on the ground to the left.

A flying bomb installation in northern France under attack.

A raid by Mosquitoes on Hirson railway yards in France has done extensive damage to locomotive sheds and repair shops as well as many of the railway tracks and carriages.

Chapter 10 - Munich

Lancasters atacked the sea defences at Walcheren at the request of the 'Underground'. The waters are pouring in to the Dutch village of WestKapelle. The targets, German troops and armour, were located nearby.

An RAF attack on coastal defences in France. The remains of a six gun battery at St Valery en Caux are outlined in white.

View from a Birdcage

Photo intelligence plotting bomb hits.

It was becoming darker very gradually, although the aircraft were still visible for several miles. We had climbed after dropping our bombs and were now at 22,000ft. It was then that I saw the mother of all explosions! A bomber had been hit with a full bomb load aboard. The cause had not been apparent; it was quite a way behind us and there was no flak at the time. A fighter could have crept in and scored a lucky hit. Alternatively, it could have been caused by another aircraft above – sadly not an uncommon occurrence now that we were nearly always carrying out saturation raids with up to 1000 bombers on one target. Anyway there it was, a small red and orange blast which multiplied at an amazing speed until it resembled the mouth of a blast furnace. Green, red and yellow flames mingled with the orange so it must have been a Pathfinder aircraft. The debris spread over a large area of the sky and gradually the flaming and glowing embers fell, glittering as they did, into a slow curve to the ground far below. All that was left in the sky was a patch of black oily smoke, drifting where moments before there had been an aircraft and

Chapter 10 - Munich

seven men. Because of the nature of the calamity no parachutes were seen.

I reported it to Ernie, and said my little prayer for them, then once again intensified my search. It had been particularly horrifying to witness the way that the bomber had disintegrated with no signs of combat or flak. My night vision was impaired for a while by the explosion and flare up, notwithstanding which I concentrated on the dark side of the sky, feeling that this was the most dangerous area for us. I heard Ernie's voice giving Emmie the new course to steer, and we turned hard to starboard and commenced our long journey home.

As things had quietened down, Frank had come back into the main part of the fuselage to give the bomb bays a visual check. This was considered necessary because although the bomb selector switches had been operated at the time that the bombs dropped, there were occasional electrical faults resulting in a bomb or bombs not being released. There was a peep hole in the floor of the fuselage immediately above the bomb bays, and Frank would be busy peering through it at this moment. In a moment or two he was back on the intercom, "One hang up Skipper, a 1,000 lb bomb on No 6 station. I'm going to get busy with the emergency toggle and see if we can lose it. Please open bomb doors". Emmie eased off the weaving and opened the bomb doors. Again the braking effect was felt as they opened into the slip stream.

It was just our luck to have a hang up, but if all went well, we should get rid of it before landing – I hoped! At least it wasn't a "Cookie". Unlike the other bombs that we carried, these Cookies were not very stable and landing with one on the aircraft was very hazardous. Frank spoke again – "It won't go, shake Willie about a bit and see if that will do it". We went into a steep dive and then flattened out, afterwards climbing nearly as steeply as we had dived. My inside felt as if it was still going down as though it was being dragged away from the rest of me. But no go – the bomb was still there! Next we slipped hard over to port, hesitated, and came diving back to starboard. Still no luck – our unwelcome cargo was still aboard. "All right" said Emmie, "We'll have another go when we are further away from the target". The bomb doors were closed and once more we settled down. We had about 200 mph showing on the clock and the target was slowly receding though it was still fairly light.

I looked around and my heart thumped wildly. There were quite a lot of aircraft to be seen but only three close enough to be recognised, two JU88s and an ME110. One of the 88s and the 110 obviously hadn't seen us, but the other certainly had. The two that hadn't were haring across the sky behind and below us, and flying at right angles to our path. They were going hell for leather towards the target area in search of potential victims. The remaining 88 was stalking quietly along, below and behind us. He was keeping the same speed as us and was just out of range of our guns. I warned Red, who hadn't seen him, the angle dead astern being too low, and the rest of the crew, asking for them to keep watch behind, sharing it with Red since the fighter had climbed a bit and was now in full view of us both. Upon reporting the fighter, Emmie had increased the steepness of the weave, making us a very difficult target to latch on to. All were now helping in the search. This had quite evidently been a fighter target, and there weren't too many pairs of eyes on Willie tonight. Suddenly the fighter pulled well back and moved out onto the starboard beam. Eventually he turned back towards us on his curve of pursuit attack. I called Emmie on the intercom "Prepare to dive starboard – dive starboard – GO". We went down in a screaming dive to starboard, and then at the bottom of the dive made an equally steep climb to port. Because of the tightness of the turn, the fighter had lost us. When next we saw him he was astern and just out of range.

Although out of range, we decided to give him a short burst. This might surprise him, though he must have known by our evasive action that we were well aware of his presence. Even if the bombs were used up, the bullets certainly weren't. Having already set up his wing span on the right sight I took aim, although our violent weaving made that extremely difficult to achieve, and almost impossible to hold for any length of time. He dived away from vision through my ring sight, and then gradually came back into it. At that precise moment my fingers tightened on the triggers, and I felt, rather than heard, the bark of the four guns, intermingled, as they were with the roar of the engines. I sensed also, that Red was firing. The smell of the cordite was pleasant and proof that my guns were working. Through my ring sight rose four curving trails of tracer from my turret, and then slowly they went down until they appeared to finish up level and slightly in front of the 88. I knew that he was out of our range, and saw him reply with his cannon. He of course was in range with his larger calibred guns, and I saw his tracer going just beneath my turret thanks largely to Emmie's weaving. All this time we had been keeping up our evasive patter. The fighter then did a side slip over to starboard. Our bursts had been quite short, maybe five seconds, but they had served the required purpose and he was even more wary

Chapter 10 - Munich

now. He may have been aware that a five second burst from six Browning guns meant that we had fired at him approximately 1200 rounds of mixed ball, armour pierce, incendiary and tracer bullets.

We continued to watch him closely, making up his mind no doubt, what form the next attack would take. A few seconds passed, then the unexpected happened. He peeled off and dived in the direction of the fast disappearing target. We confirmed this with the rest of the crew, and once more we settled down to a more gentle weave. We had all been sure that on this occasion we were due for a prolonged combat, with the possibility of one or other of us getting the chop! Instead, other than the odd pass or two, he had apparently been disturbed by the fact that we were wide awake, and prepared to have a go. Probably our brief burst of fire had made the decision for him. The final result was a bit of an anti-climax, though we had no complaints.

The cold began to penetrate. Only then did I realise that at the commencement of the combat I had automatically turned off the heat. I quickly turned it on again, and gradually some feeling crept back again into my limbs. The sky to port was still fairly light, faintly illuminated by the fast disappearing target now many miles behind. Once again our search concentration was to the starboard and darker side of the sky. We were back over the very mountainous country of Southern Germany and Austria, somewhere between Munich and Lake Constance on the Swiss border. If we were to be shot down our chances of escape would be negligible, indeed the chop was an almost foregone conclusion. On the other hand, in the event of a crash landing and a miraculous escape, the Swiss border would be fairly handy, giving us at least a fighting chance to get through.

Not too far from where we now were was a well known escape route for aircrew on the run in this part of Germany. This was the Schaffhausen salient, very close to the German town of Singen. The salient was formed by a very narrow neck of Swiss territory protruding into the Third Reich like a finger of land. Aircrew on the run in the vicinity of Switzerland invariably made for this geographical feature. If one were lucky enough to reach it, one had to exercise great care after crossing the Swiss border, not too cross right over this narrow strip of territory and find oneself back in Germany!

I hoped that soon we should see the lights of Switzerland. Only once since the commencement of war had we seen a lit city from the air. This had been on the occasion that we were on a raid at Stettin. We were stooging along over the Skaggerak off the eastern coast of Denmark, and had been enthralled by the sight of Swedish cities, Malmo in particular, glittering in the velvet blackness; a never to be forgotten sight.

A big flash flared up behind us somewhere in the region of the target. Probably the fire that had been spreading and had reached a store of petroleum or explosives. It was big enough to note and I passed on the information to Ernie. His log was going to be full of incidents that night. It was from such information, probably supplied and confirmed by many aircraft, that a fuller picture of the raid and its probable success could be built up.

In spite of the cold I began to feel drowsy. We had been flying for well over four hours and there was still at least another four hours to go before we touched down at base. Despite my weariness, I knew that I should be able to remain awake, fear being a great spur against lassitude. Harry was talking to Emmie. He'd seen five aircraft ahead of us get the chop while we had been running up onto the target. Since we were so early on in the attack, and because of the number of fighters that I had seen milling around, I feared that our total losses would be high bearing in mind that there were several hundred bombers in the attack on this target, the bulk of which had been behind us. Hopefully the attack had been successful, since apart from his initial call, we had not heard the Master Bomber giving any correction to the initial aiming point.

Red called me and asked if there were any activity down at my end. My eyes were strained from trying to pierce the dark side of the sky, but all seemed quiet in that direction. Soon now there wouldn't be a lighter side to the sky since the glare from the target had almost gone. Beneath us thin wisps of cloud were slowly drifting by, but at our level it continued to remain clear.

I thought once again, of the hang up in the bomb bay. It was a pity that it hadn't shaken loose during our earlier manoeuvres. We had carried it a long way and had no desire to take it back with us to England. I felt sure that we should eventually get rid of it, preferably before we crossed the German border - fortunately there was a lot of Hun territory remaining. Harry checked the petrol consumption, something that he had been doing regularly throughout the trip. Old Willie was doing well; he had plenty in hand and everything was running smoothly. The oil temperature was running a bit high on one engine, but nothing to cause undue alarm and a careful watch could be maintained on that engine.

We had a lot of faith in our aircraft, having flown it on nearly all of

Chapter 10 - Munich

our operations to date, and we felt that we knew each other well. A few months earlier we had had an engine failure when on operations to Mainz. In the event, the failure of this engine seemed to have made little difference to Willie's performance. The only noticeable variation was that it took a little longer to climb to our operational height, otherwise the performance seemed to remain the same and Willie seemed to be quite content on the three remaining Merlins.

The cold was even more intense and I discovered an icicle 5 inches long on my oxygen mask, and I had to put a finger into the outlet to break it off. I threw it into the slipstream. Without any warning we dived very steeply to starboard. At first I thought that Emmie was making another attempt to get rid of the bomb, then realised that this could not be so because nothing had been said on the intercom, nor had I felt the bomb bay doors opening. I swung the turret round to see if there was anything to account for the sudden manoeuvre, but saw nothing. The intercom came alive and Emmie said, "JU88 on the starboard bow – watch out for him, he'll be moving astern directly." Instantly, I swung round ready for him as soon as he came within sight and range. We had reached the bottom of the corkscrew and were climbing to port. I still remember my initial thoughts when this attack so suddenly commenced... "What a clot! Attacking us from the front, and the lighter side of the sky." Red ought to get a good picture of him as he came round onto the beam, and I should see him shortly afterwards. We were now at the top of our manoeuvre and commenced to dive when I heard Red open up. As yet the fighter hadn't come into my vision, the starboard fin and rudder keeping him from my sight. All the intercoms were now live. I heard Red give him another burst, and as he altered his deflection, continued with short bursts. Emmie came through again - "He's still firing. I believe he's hit us somewhere down in the front". Red was firing continuously and Frank had managed to get a few bursts off from the front turret. I still waited anxiously for him to come round into a position from which I could fire. After a life–time of waiting, he at last appeared in my sight. He was within about 300 yards of our quarter and appeared to be firing at us without a break. Fortunately Emmie's manoeuvres were spot on and his shots were going under and astern of my turret. I got him lined up making the essential deflection allowances and commenced firing, continuously. The 88 stopped firing, but Red and I continued with long bursts. Slowly, he moved round to the back of us, starboard quarter, fine quarter, dead astern. At dead astern we were both firing at him point blank, a no deflection shot. I could almost feel our bullets going into him, then we commenced climbing, and the deflection altered rapidly until it was almost impossible to keep him in the ring sight. He moved back now, and was out of our range, and then dived down under us. For a minute or two we were left in peace, then back he came for another attack. During the whole of the time Emmie had been doing a shattering corkscrew, and when, briefly we levelled out, we wondered whether we had seen the last of him – but no such luck! He came in fast from starboard, in the usual curve of pursuit, trying at the same time to match our evasive action. Just before he came into range we managed to get in a hurried "Dive Starboard – GO". Instantly we dived very steeply, and as he gradually came astern of us we both opened up.

Again it seemed that we were hitting him, in so much as our tracer bullets appeared to be going into the nose and wing roots of the 88. However it had been proved beyond doubt that optical illusions were not infrequent when trying to assess tracer bullets, and at 400 yards, bullets which appeared to be hitting the aircraft might really be curving away and in fact passing just in front or behind the target. Because of this optical illusion, at a later date instructions came from Group that all Pathfinder squadrons would cease to use tracer bullets.

The 88 again broke away beneath us without scoring any more hits on Willie, nor had we caused any apparent damage to the fighter, although I wondered because his last manoeuvres had seemed very sloppy - almost as though he might be having control problems. Once more he came into sight, high on our port side, again out of range but keeping station with us. He continued to do so for a few seconds, then dived down and moved to the limits of our vision, at least half a mile away. He was no longer firing, though we were just within his range, and appeared content to keep us in sight. At this range his cannon could have reached us, though he would need to adopt another curve of pursuit attack for he knew that as soon as he commenced firing we should again take violent evasive action. At this time he was merely keeping station, perhaps thinking of some new ruse which would offer him a greater chance of success than those that which he had so far employed.

Suddenly, he switched on his nav lights. For a moment we thought that he had been joined by another fighter, so accordingly we all gave a lot of attention on the other side away from him. Seconds passed and nothing untoward happened, then just as quickly his lights went out and he curved round from port to commence another attack. At the appropriate moment

Chapter 10 - Munich

we gave Emmie the evasive action to take, and once again we did a stomach lifting dive and corkscrew. He came in firing, and turned away perilously close to my turret and the fin and rudder. The shots that he had fired were way off and ours had fared no better thanks to our prompt and violent dive which was more than enough to make us an extremely difficult target to hit, or for us to score on him. During the action that we in the turrets had just taken, we had perhaps only a second when he was a point blank shot. After this moment had passed we fired continuously with a hose pipe effect. On the last of this attack I thought that I had seen some small pieces break away from his nose. We commenced our climb, having turned inside the fighter curve, and he vanished from our sight.

He was missing for about 30 seconds, then suddenly he shot overhead and Harry reported that he seemed to be coming around to make another head on attack. This time Frank stayed in the nose and as soon as the attack commenced, he fired long bursts at the rapidly closing fighter. Again I had to wait for him to come round and appear in my sight. Red in the meantime was firing steadily. He soon came into my view and I commenced firing steadily. He had by now reached the port quarter and suddenly I saw a series of sparks run along his fuselage, showing that we were hitting him. Suddenly he did a half roll and dived down straight behind us, dead astern. I still had him in my sight and continued firing though he was at extreme range. It was fascinating to watch his power dive down towards the earth. I felt sure that we had got him, either the pilot himself or some vital part of the aircraft.

There was no visible flame at about the time that he would have crashed, but the cloud beneath us had thickened considerably, and from experience we also knew that there were occasions when an aircraft crashed without bursting into flames. From the time that he had last been positioned astern he had not returned our fire, but had just turned over to port, and then gone straight down in what appeared to be an uncontrollable dive.

Emmie had now ceased the corkscrew and had gone back into a nice steady weave and once more we were on course for England. Harry said he was going down into the nose to ascertain whether we had been hit, and if so, what damage might have been sustained. Since the commencement Willie had behaved perfectly normally, much to our relief. During the whole of the recent combat Nobby had followed the JU88 on "Fishpond", our downward seeing radar. This set gave coverage of approximately 180° from below the aircraft and down to ground level. He had watched the fighter diving down to earth finally vanishing at deck level never to reappear. This was proof positive, as far as we were concerned, that he had crashed. Some hours later when we were talking over the combat, Red and I decided to share the kill. We had both fired continuously and we both had almost certainly scored hits. It was impossible for either of us to know who had been directly responsible for bringing down the fighter.

Harry came back with the news that we had been hit! It appeared that a cannon shell, judging by the size of the hole, had come through the nose on the port side without exploding: in passing it had hit and burst an emergency oxygen bottle, and had also damaged the bomb sight computer, continuing on out of the other side of the aircraft. Since the shell had failed to burst, the fighter must have been very close to have done that damage. For us it was a very lucky shot, because one cannon shell in the wrong place, particularly as they normally exploded on impact, would have been quite capable of bringing down the aircraft or igniting the fuel. As it was, we'd just had a delayed scare, none more so than Frank and Harry who had both left the nose of the aircraft only a short while before we had been hit. We discovered afterwards that the same shell had penetrated the port inner engine cowling en route, again with no damage to the engine.

Quietness descended on Willie once more, but with very watchful eyes from all the crew. It was still clear and unspeakably cold. I mulled over the recent attacks and came to the conclusion that we had been very unlucky to have been involved with a second JU88. Long experience had shown that the average night fighter pilot, when he found a potential victim, came in for the attack, but if he met with return fire he usually broke off the engagement after one pass at the bomber and went in search of another less wide awake crew. Thus the average fighter pilot showed that he too had an inbred sense of self preservation. Our late adversary was obviously of another ilk, being prepared to fight to the death which he undoubtedly had achieved. Below us the clouds were now solid, and building up slowly to our level. The glow from the target had long since gone, though sometimes there was an occasional lightning in that area which indicated that explosions were still taking place, probably delayed action bombs and spreading fires, because the raid had finished a long time ago. We had also seen three combats taking place behind us. They had been too far behind us to recognise the aircraft involved or to see any results.

Again I was being troubled by the extreme cold and thought longingly of my flask of coffee. Fifteen to twenty miles to port a searchlight had suddenly erupted into the sky. There was no wavering and no flak, it just pointed straight up. This would almost certainly be a night fighter beacon. The fighters orbited this light while waiting for instructions from their ground control. We weren't headed that way so there was no point in reporting it.

Steadily we forged ahead, making occasional corrections to our course. Harry said that the lights of a Swiss town were moving up on the beam and that I should see them soon. Frank reminded Emmie of the hang up and it was decided to have another go at losing the bomb. "Bomb doors open" said Frank. "Bomb doors opening" said Emmie. The shudder followed and ceased as soon as they were fully open. I gripped the side members of the turret and waited for it. "Diving" said the Skipper. Down we went into a screaming dive, way down, and then pulled out of it. It felt as though Willie was hanging onto the sky with his propellers. My stomach took long seconds to catch up with me. At the end of the very steep climb we levelled off and Frank went back to see if we had been successful. Again – no go! The unwelcome passenger was still with us. Once more we tried and must have dropped several thousand feet in an incredibly few seconds. During that dive I found that I was glued to the roof of the turret, something that Emmie had never before subjected me to. The four lines of ammunition belts feeding the guns rose before my eyes, suspended in mid air as if by magic. This time when we pulled out, I had almost to will my stomach to stay with me. The steepness of this dive had been such that I doubt if any lesser aircraft than the Lancaster would have retained it's wings!

Having levelled out Frank went back to investigate. Back came his voice – "OK, bomb gone". The bomb doors closed and we all peered below. A few moments later we saw a bright flash as our late unlamented cargo hit the earth. Although we were over a very desolate area, it seemed likely that someone would have had the shock of their lives. I doubt if any bomb had ever been dropped in that area before.

Over to port, Switzerland slowly passed by. Some way off on the far side of Lake Constance was a town, quite small I believe, but its shops and house windows sprawled about in a sparkling array, shimmering on a purple background. There were moving gems that must have been the headlights of cars throwing swathes of light in all directions. I had eventually to tear my eyes away from this fascinating scene. I feared

View from a Birdcage

that if I continued to watch it some Hun might come creeping in from the darkness. All remained quiet as we continued our search, with an occasional glance at the fast receding Swiss town. Very gradually this fascinating sight faded and became lost in the distance until finally it was nothing but a memory to be cherished on many a dismal night in the future.

As if to mock this peaceful sight, yet another cluster of fighter flares were dropped, slightly below our level, and thankfully a few miles off. They hung in the sky like six white mushrooms, throwing off a pale but all revealing light, dropping molten globs of fire as their parachutes slowly lowered them to the earth. A few miles ahead another six dropped, probably from the same aircraft. So far it was apparent that no contact had been made with any of our bombers, but in the pale light between the flares that were astern and ourselves, I could see one lone Lancaster doing a steady weave, slowly forging ahead towards the French frontier. Nothing further happened. The flares receded slowly astern, until eventually they burnt themselves out and all was quiet.

Shortly afterwards, Ernie gave an alteration of course to starboard, and we turned in the direction of Strasbourg, close to the German/French frontier. This would be followed by a long stooge across France to the Channel, and thence home, glorious home. It was about now that the cloud commenced to build up to our level, patchy at first becoming increasingly thick. I had a brief natter with Nobby and Red and gave Ernie some of the gen on combats that I had seen around the target area. Red estimated that he had fired some 1,200 rounds of ammunition during our last combat. Since we had fired for approximately the same amount of time, and allowing for the fact that I had double the fire power, we must have put, jointly, about 3,600 rounds in the fighter's direction. To this must be added several hundred rounds fired at him from the front turret. Ernie was working steadily on the navigation problems with Frank's assistance. The work required all of his concentration and only on rare occasions did he have the opportunity for a natter. We all appreciated old Ernie – he was a fine navigator. I sent over my usual jibe at Frank's expense, asking if the Nav team were gorging themselves while the poor rear gunner sat starving and freezing to death in the rear turret. A few trips before we had learned that he and Ernie had a big feast while on operations. A large tin of tongue figured in this banquet, part of a food parcel for him from his parents in New Zealand. Both he and Ernie used to receive regular food parcels from home, and many a party our crew had had in the billet as a result of these goodies from overseas. On this particular trip in question, Frank had a feeling that he was going to be hungry so he took with him part of the contents of a recently arrived food parcel. On the trip back they really enjoyed themselves. Under the conditions that we were flying, it would have been quite impossible for them to have passed back anything to me in the tail end, but I had taken the opportunity of pulling Frank's leg about the incident ever since.

We were now drawing close to the French frontier and Emmie said that we were just about to enter very thick cloud ahead of us. We couldn't get above it, as the estimated tops were not less than 30,000 feet. At the moment we were at 22,000 feet and to climb much higher would use too much valuable fuel, even if we could make that height which was doubtful. A few minutes later we were back in the grey icy fog. Hopefully, combats could be forgotten now, but there were equally unpleasant things to cope with. I began to feel increasingly fatigued and miserable and once again tried singing to raise my spirits. I could now, with safety, have taken my coffee, but on principle decided to leave it to the usual time when we crossed the coast of good old England. Once more ice was building up all over the aircraft, though I could only see it on the fins, rudders and aerials from my position. The temperature was still around 50 degrees below, and I hoped (in vain as it proved) that we should never again experience a temperature this low.

Emmie dived the aircraft and managed to break off some of the ice from the main plane. We levelled off again, and for a few precious minutes flew in a clear lane between two layers of cloud then we were back again in the midst of it. After some problems, Frank thought that he had got a good fix on Gee and said that we were now crossing the German/French frontier. This meant the possibility of friends below us once more – a nice comforting thought. We seemed to be maintaining very good time despite the diversions we suffered as a result of the two combats and the vagaries of very changeable weather. I realised, suddenly, that in this huge bank of cloud there were several hundred other bombers spread out for miles astern. The static on the radio was becoming very bad, but for a few minutes, Nobby picked up and held some late dance music from somewhere on the continent. They were playing "The St Louis Blues", and for a few minutes we held a lively chorus. This cheered me up a lot, and for a while I forgot my tiredness and aching limbs. Harry was making up his log and all was well with Willie and his engines. We had bombed only five seconds late, and successfully foiled the hated Hun – though not

View from a Birdcage

without a few mental scars. Altogether, the trip could be called a winner – so far. Briefly we passed through a clear patch, and I caught sight of a twinkling light far below, our first sight of France for several hours.

Ernie and Frank were having trouble in finding a good wind. It seemed to have increased speed quite dramatically and Gee was not proving as reliable as it usually was. Ernie gave a small alteration to port. As we slowly turned I caught sight of another Lanc above us on our beam. His four engine exhaust were glowing in the gloom. I warned Emmie, but the aircraft was on a slightly different course and moving away from us. Soon it was out of sight. Shortly afterwards we were back in cloud with increasing turbulence. The recent encounter with our compatriot had made us very wary and I tried to pierce the surrounding cloud making my eyes ache in the process. We saw nothing else although there were undoubtedly many bombers around us. We were icing up steadily, and slowly but surely the icy atmosphere was working its way into my limbs. Breaking the ice off the oxygen mask was now a continuous process, as was regular blinking to stop my eyelashes from freezing together.

Happily we again came into a clear patch, and the indications were that it might last for a while. There was still thin cloud below and nothing could be seen of the ground; however, we could see all around us which made life easier and marginally warmer. I cast a quick look around for other bombers or fighters but all was very quiet. Nobby fiddled about for a while on the receiver trying to get some more music to cheer us up, but the static was too bad and he eventually gave it up. We were too late for the last BBC news. On several occasions in the past we had picked up the late news bulletin and listened to the first details of a raid in which we had just played a part in fact while we were still on our way home from that particular raid.

Nobby came on again. He'd just picked up a broadcast from Group. Morse transmission was not so badly affected by static as plain language. The message was a warning to the effect that bandits were about in East Anglia, and in the area in which our airfield was situated. "Bandits" was the Service term for marauding German night fighters. They were stooging around our landing fields hoping to shoot some of us down as we came back from the raid. It would still be a long time before we were back over England, so there wasn't much to worry about so far as we were concerned although the Mosquitos which had been helping us earlier in the raid, because of their very much higher speed, would be approaching the airfields for landing and would therefore be taking

Chapter 10 - Munich

serious note of the warning. The bright idea of attacking bombers as they landed at their base emanated from the Royal Air Force earlier in the war and we still engaged in these forays on occasions, usually using Mosquitos equipped with cannon. Quite a measure of success had been achieved. The Luftwaffe had eventually cottoned on to the idea but for some reason had not obtained the same good results as ourselves; in fact we considered them as having only a minor nuisance value. Our radar and other defences were on the top line and rather spoiled things for them. If the bandits were still around when we got back to our airfield, which I doubted, it would be necessary for us to remain extra vigilant right up to the time that we were to land. There would not be the usual relaxation that we normally enjoyed after crossing our coast on the journey home.

We were now flying completely free of cloud at our level, but there were massive banks above us and still complete cloud cover below. Emmie said that it would probably be OK for the rest of the journey home; the "front" was now behind us. The temperature had gone up a little, and although it was probably still close to 50 below, even a very slight improvement worked wonders for the spirit. We continued our search in the clear layer, and once briefly caught a fleeting glimpse of the ground which vanished from our sight just as quickly. We had the usual bonus of seeing the ice gradually going. A long way ahead there was a faint diffused light from a searchlight battery and some light flak just broke cloud below. We should be well above it when we passed that area. With the improvement in conditions generally, I felt more comfortable although I was having the usual combat against fatigue. By now we had been flying for nearly six hours and drowsiness was an increasing danger. So far as I was aware, never once on any trip had I allowed my eyes to close from fatigue, but the fear of this happening was very real and ever present. The thought of an attack whilst my eyes were closed was a vital stimulant in helping me to keep awake.

We weaved steadily onwards, not as steeply as we had when over Germany but sufficient to prevent us from becoming a sitting duck in the event of a sudden surprise attack. It was possible for us to be able to make a good search underneath the aircraft. Ernie spoke again, still complaining of continuing difficulties in assessing the winds. They were much stronger than he had anticipated, and once more he gave a new course to steer.

I could hear Red bitching about the draught in the back of his neck. I felt sure that he would willingly have spent the whole day crawling about inside Willie with a tin of putty to fill up all the cracks and crevices. The draught that caused the most trouble had been traced to the flare chute, just aft of his turret. He had tried everything to make it draught proof, without any conspicuous success. A little later activity commenced once more. We ran over a small flak battery somewhere in the wilds of France. Unlike the earlier battery we had seen, this was a battery of heavy flak – all 88s. A few seconds later several bursts of flak arrived. One shell was near enough to be unpleasant, and a small fragment of the shell hit us just aft of the entrance hatch, quite close to the Master Repeater compass. We didn't discover this until after we had landed, although at the time Red had said that he had heard it hit us. It must have been quite a small battery, but apart from the initial surprise and lucky shot they hadn't bothered us much. In the reflection of the accompanying searchlights I had seen a Halifax and another Lancaster.

We now had a little over an hour to go before crossing the French coast. Nobby picked up the "All clear" message from Group – the bandits had left the area. We heard later that they were just two lone raiders making a general nuisance of themselves. They had no success other than to cause general alarm. One had been in the general vicinity of our own airfield and our ground defences had pooped off a couple of bursts, apparently with no effect other than to give the air defences some sorely needed practice and to brighten their lives a little!

I helped myself to my last piece of chewing gum, thinking happily that the next time that I opened my mouth to put anything in it, it would be hot glorious coffee. Thinking about it, I picked up the flask and tried the cap. It was frozen solid from the condensation inside the container. I managed to unzip a few inches of my outer flying suit and with difficulty put the flask inside so that my body heat would thaw it out – or so I hoped – by the time I was ready to use it. The minutes passed slowly. Somewhere on our port side, about level with us, lay Paris but not a glimmer of light was to be seen. If we were lucky the only activity that we could now expect would be when we crossed the coast when it was the usual practice for the guns and searchlights to give us parting salvos. This ranged from a few desultory bursts to a veritable barrage. The latter only if we were unwise enough to be off course, perhaps in the vicinity of Calais, Dunquerque or Boulogne or some such heavily defended area. These coastal defences were quite horrendous and had been responsible for shooting down many British and Allied aircraft. Depending upon where we actually crossed the coast, the defences would range from a few spasmodic bursts to a

Chapter 10 - Munich

horrifying cloud of steel fragments as heavy as any over major German cities. Of course, the flight plans studiously avoided crossing such areas, so it was up to the Navigator, and luck, to make sure that such hazards were avoided. Many an aircraft got thus far on its return from a successful raid and then fell victim, at the last minute, to these intense barrages.

Earlier on in the war there had been a very large concentration of German fighter airfields stretching along the coasts of France, Belgium and Holland. During the previous year, most of these airfields had received regular batterings from the RAF and USAF. Mainly due to this prolonged hammering, air recce had shown that the majority of the German squadrons had been withdrawn to their home based airfields, or to occupied countries close to their borders. The reasons were twofold – the aforementioned battering that they had received, and the urgent need to counteract the massive bombing of the Third Reich by the Allies. The comparatively few remaining fighter airfields were harassed by Mosquitos on an almost daily basis. Also joining in the attacks were Tempests and Typhoons of Fighter Command. Thus it was quite rare these days for returning Allied bombers to be unduly bothered by fighters when crossing the Belgian and French coasts.

It continued to remain quiet and we hoped that it would stay that way. We'd had more than our quota of action for that night, and I for one was prepared to settle down and enjoy a nice monotonous end to our trip. By now we must have been about a hundred miles from the coast. The winds seemed to have veered again and seemed to be more in our favour, so hopefully we shouldn't be late back at base. I thought of the eggs, bacon and chips waiting for us back in the Mess to be followed by bed, glorious bed! If luck were to be with us we might have the following night off. If we had been out two nights on the trot, as we now had, we usually got a "stand down", though there were occasional exceptions. If we weren't flying, Frank would certainly be seeing his girlfriend, Christine. I should accompany him on this pleasant night out, since my girlfriend Eileen was Christine's sister. At the end of the war, a year or so hence, Christine went out to New Zealand and married Frank and had a fine family. My war time romance with Eileen ended when I was posted away from Downham Market at the end of hostilities.

Our social life on the Squadron, when flying allowed, was most enjoyable, not the least because of our many friends in the small country town. Foremost of these were Ron and Marjorie Bennett and their charming family. Ron was a farmer and the family had adopted our crew.

View from a Birdcage

Their home at Bridge Farm was an ever open door. One just arrived, often without any warning, and were immediately made welcome. Marjorie soon learned of my great weakness – home made chocolate cake – and there was always one awaiting my arrival. Their friendship and hospitality was treasured by us all, as was the similar hospitality offered by Vic and Queenie Bennett, Ron's brother and sister in law.

Myself with Rosemarie Bennett. Along with her husband, Ron, she made our crew very welcome at Bridge Farm

Chapter 10 - Munich

Downham Market. Take off showing Bridge Farm.

Downham Market 1944. On my old Sunbeam.

In front and behind us there was now not a cloud to be seen above or below our level, and the stars were twinkling coldly. This sudden clearance above and below us was quite unexpected, but it didn't last for long. The cloud soon built up again, though at our level we remained in the clear. Again there was a very brief clearance below us, and for a moment I caught sight of a river. I asked Ernie which river it was, and he replied "Probably the Seine". The lack of opposition continued and Harry confirmed that all was quiet ahead of us.

Our luck continued to hold good. Five minutes went by, ten minutes, and still all was peaceful. Some minutes later Emmie said that there was some light flak ahead, just above the cloud top. Ernie said that it could be one of the coastal batteries. As he said this, the heavy flak opened up. Fortunately we were well to port and due to cross the coast in a few minutes. Almost immediately Frank got a good fix, since providentially the cloud below had commenced to clear. Within minutes we were crossing the beaches and on our last lap. As I looked over to the heavy flak only a few miles away, I saw an enormous explosion at our level. There was thick black oily smoke with orange and red flames. It had the appearance of being a direct hit with a full bomb load, but all the aircraft now crossing the coast would be empty of bombs. The consensus of opinion amongst us was that it had probably been a scarecrow. This was believed to be an anti-aircraft shell devised to simulate a bomber exploding, and intended as a psychological deterrent. Similar devices had been reported on many occasions when it had been confirmed that in fact that there were no aircraft in the immediate vicinity of the explosion. They were normally fired in the target area, and this was the first occasion that we had seen one fired when crossing the coast.

Plenty of searchlights and flak continued to harass the bomber behind us. No fighters had appeared, and in view of the gun fire it was unlikely that any would be around for as long as the intense barrage continued. Flak never bothers you until one has had the experience of being badly hit, as had happened to us on several occasions. From then onwards it seems to have a very personal touch about it! Consequently it is thereafter treated with a great deal of fear and respect.

We were still weaving, and in the reflection of the searchlights I saw that we were in the company of another Lancaster. He was about a hundred feet above us and weaving in the other direction to ourselves. Every 15 seconds we'd swoosh by each other as we dived in opposite directions. Once we were so close that I could see the Captain of the

Chapter 10 - Munich

other Lanc giving us the thumbs up. I tried hard to decipher the squadron letters, thinking that maybe it was one of our own aircraft, but the reflected light was not quite bright enough. Although we were by now about a mile out to sea, a searchlight came full onto us and I felt like the proverbial gold fish in a glass bowl a very naked feeling. I kept my eyes away from the source of the beam, noticing, at the same time that our companion of a few minutes before had managed to dive away into the darkness. Emmie put us into a steep dive to port. As we went down the flak came up and burst directly in front of where our original course could well have been. Vicious looking orange bursts – six of them. They had been very well predicted, bursting more or less in a straight line one after the other in rapid succession. We straightened out of the dive, and as we did so the searchlight flickered and went out, leaving us once more in friendly darkness. I breathed normally once more and gave a little prayer of thanks.

Since entering the recent flak area I had adopted my usual hunched up position, and now relaxed. This was an instinctive position that I always assumed when caught by searchlights. It was of course a feeble attempt, subconscious at that, to make oneself a smaller target. Not much point at all really, but as already said, quite instinctive. We were now well clear of the beach area and I was able to watch the firework display in a more or less disinterested manner. Another aircraft behind us had been coned in the lights, but he was less lucky than we had been. He had about six searchlights on him, and despite a hair raising display of aerobatics the lights continued to hold him. After a minute or two he was in trouble. Up came the flak, very accurately, and he was hit. A small glow developed in the centre of the fuselage and heavy smoke was pouring out. I guessed that it was probably from the hydraulic oil feeding the turrets and ammunition racks. By this time he was just away from the beach and losing height rapidly, though in a fairly well controlled dive. Possibly he was diving deliberately, because this was the way that small fires could sometimes be extinguished. As soon as the flak batteries saw that he was in trouble, they redoubled their efforts, throwing everything up at him, though apparently without scoring any more hits. Then the lights left him expecting, no doubt, that the bomber would crash. Accordingly, he was left to his own salvation. He was, by now, down to about 5,000ft and as far as one could tell about eight miles out to sea. The fire was no worse and I began to think that he would make the English coast after all. There was an emergency landing field at RAF Manston, close by Ramsgate, which was of great use to aircraft in trouble. In fact, since the ending of the Battle of Britain, emergency landings were its main purpose. The pilot of the bomber obviously had this in mind, and had altered course directly for Manston, now only a short distance away from his present position. Had he kept onto the original course that we all had to follow, he would have had to travel another 50 miles or so over the sea. As it was he had now reduced it to well under 20 miles, no more than seven minutes flying time. The Lancaster vanished from sight and I mentally wished them well.

Again peace had descended on us. The searchlights and guns had faded into the distance, and apart from a very slight risk of prowling night fighters, it seemed that the night's excitement might be at an end. Emmie said that we had about another fifteen minutes to go before crossing our coast. I smacked my lips at the thought of the flask nestling between my inner and outer suits. We were now losing height quite rapidly and were down to about 14,000ft. At this level the temperature had improved a lot, and for the first time in a good many hours I began to feel warmer and reasonably comfortable. The fatigue also seemed to have left me and I was able to maintain a very wide awake search, happy in the knowledge that those eggs and bacon would soon be within my grasp, and the delectable bed shortly afterwards.

Harry sighted a beacon flashing from an English airfield, proof that there were no German night fighters about. The estimate was that we should be crossing the English coast within five minutes. Emmie flattened out the weave and we settled down to flying straight and level for the first time in over six hours. Once more Emmie spoke "Down to 10,000ft, Oxygen off". Thankfully I detached the oxygen tube and breathed great gulps of natural air. This in turn banished any remaining tiredness that I felt. "Coast coming up" said Harry, and a minute later we were over the cliffs of Beachy Head.

"Navigation lights on". A moment passed then on came the welcome gleam of our wing tip and tail lights. The great moment had arrived. I fumbled about with my outer suit, found the zip, pulled it down and felt for the flask. It took some finding, having got well down beneath the level of the parachute harness on top. Triumphantly, my fingers closed over the cup and I withdrew it from its cache. We were still descending, quite quickly now that we were over England, and there was a correspondingly rapid increase in the temperature. I was therefore able to take off two pairs of gloves to facilitate removing the cup from the top of the flask. I

Chapter 10 - Munich

gave it a good hearty grip, twisted, and nothing happened! I increased my grip and tried again – still nothing happened. Switching on the red drift scale light, I held the flask in its dull glow. Right round the edge of the cup, where it screwed into the flask, was a solid ring of ice despite the fact that it had been encased in my suit for a long time. Wasting not a second, I fumbled in my knee pocket and found my knife. Chipping vigorously I soon removed the ice, and at the next attempt the cup unscrewed. It was as well that the weaving had stopped, for it would have been difficult to have kept any liquid in the cup under those conditions.

I removed the cork and the hot steaming smell of coffee reached my nose. Filling the cup three quarters full, I drank. It tasted like the finest nectar to my parched mouth and throat. I mentally wallowed in joy, and felt at peace with the world. It was not only the coffee, but also what it symbolised – we were back over England with another trip successfully completed. I busied myself with a second cup, a third, and then a fourth, until finally the flask was empty. I burped gently, a combination of coffee on an empty stomach and constantly chewing gum. Replacing the flask in the corner of the turret, I called Emmie "Rear Gunner here Skip. Can I lock and centralise the turret and lay back in the fuselage for a stretch?" Back came the reply "OK, Rear Gunner. Mid Upper, keep a sharp look out while Jack's having his stretch". I locked the turret in the fore and aft position, and opening the sliding doors behind me with my elbows, I lay back and stretched – Joy of Joys! I could have purred, but after a couple of minutes of sheer delight I clambered back into the turret, informed Emmie, then unlocked the turret and resumed the search.

By now we were some 20 miles inland, and behind us I could see a large number of aircraft following us home, plainly visible now that we all had our lights on. Below and around us beacons were flashing on many airfields. As yet we had not reached Bomber Country, so no landing lights were switched on. By now we were down to 5,000 feet, and wonder of wonders, I actually felt warm! The outside temperature had gone up to just above zero, and I reached out to turn off the heating to my gloves and suit. Ernie called up and gave an estimated time of arrival at base and Nobby got busy contacting the airfield, giving them this information. We were approaching the last turning point and in a minute or two we should be heading directly to Downham Market, reaching there in about 35 minutes time. Despite the "all clear" message that we had received regarding the Bandits, we were still keeping a good lookout against surprise attack. With everyone having their lights on, and with the skies now completely clear there was little chance of collision with other aircraft, and shortly we should split up into many different streams heading for our respective airfields.

We turned sharply to starboard and the last leg home commenced. Below us in the darkness lay the big industrial town of Reading. Not a glimmer of light showed itself – the blackout was complete. I wondered if the folks below had become used to the route of many hundreds of bombers going out over them, and some hours later repeating the flight inbound, each time using their town as a turning point. Up here in the solitude, and with the noise of our engines constant over many hours, they were by reason of familiarity unheard by us.

Again a feeling of drowsiness came over me, but not the desperate freezing tiredness that I had experienced over Germany some hours before. This was a warm contented feeling, engendered in part by thoughts of comparative freedom from danger, of being back safely, and of the food and comfortable bed soon to be enjoyed. It was quite a different type of fatigue and very much easier to combat.

For some reason I began to think of the strange way we had all been thrown together, and how we had grown from being seven strangers into a completely integrated and smoothly working crew, trusting each other completely and combined with a feeling of comradeship that could not have been surpassed had we been trained, worked and lived together for years instead of the few months that it had actually been. Yet here we were, with little more than eight months behind us, just completing our fortieth operation. A tight bond indeed!

My thoughts were interrupted by an airfield below switching on the outer circuit lights, yellow and gleaming. The ring of lights were several miles in circumference and incorporated a funnel of lights leading out of them, and pointing in the direction of the runway in use. Below I could see a Lancaster travelling around the circuit prior to landing. The airfield below was another Pathfinder station, RAF Gravely in Huntingdon. In another 10 minutes we should be doing the same procedure. An attack of cramp made my thighs twitch, and having obtained the Skipper's OK, I fumbled behind me, found the turret latches and opened the doors and lay down, half in the turret and half out. Once again I wallowed in luxury. The cramp went almost immediately, and I had to drag myself back into the turret before I fell asleep.

On our port wing another Lancaster was formatting us. In the reflection from some landing lights from a nearby airfield, I could just

Chapter 10 - Munich

make out our Squadron markings; it was one of our own crews. I spoke to Red, "Who was in J Johnnie tonight?" Back came the reply, "I think it was Alec; why?" I said "He's formatting on our port wing. It looks as if he is trying to nip in ahead of us - trying to pip us on the post for landing". There was a very strict code of honour amongst aircrew which was that we did not call up Flying Control until actually crossing our outer circuit lights. The rule was, first home, first to land, and in the last few minutes of flying time it was not unusual for all of our aircraft to be pretty well bunched together, all hoping to be first to touch down. This code was strictly adhered to, but excluded any aircraft in difficulties or having fuel problems.

For a few minutes J Johnnie stayed with us, then moved out to port, gradually disappearing from our sight. We passed over two more lighted airfields, RAF Waterbeach and Mepal, then saw dimly the two long straight canals which confirmed that we were heading directly for base, and should be arriving in a few minutes time. Frank was the first to see it, dead ahead, a continuous red flashing beacon in morse- D.O, D.O, D.O, our recognition letters of the day.

Emmie had the R.T switched on, ready for calling up Flying Control. Then we heard the first aircraft over the airfield boundary calling up "Hello Offstrike, Hello Offstrike this is Cut Out X Ray, this is Cut Out X Ray". The reply came back promptly "Hello Cut Out X Ray, hello Cut Out X Ray, this is Offstrike, this is Offstrike prepare to land, turn left, out".

I could see the outer circuit lights now. Emmie began calling – "Hello Offs – ", then he was pipped on the post by K King, only a few hundred yards ahead of us. As soon as he had finished and had received his landing instructions, Emmie jumped in and completed his call. Back came the reply – "Hello Cut Out Willie, Hello Cut Out Willie – turn three, turn three, 3,000, out". We were third to land, which was fair enough. Slowly we circled base at 3,000ft, preparing to be called down to land as soon as the two aircraft ahead of us had landed. The sky was very clear and completely cloudless. Above us some more of our aircraft had joined the circuit and were stacked at 1,000ft intervals. They too were circling, awaiting their turn. We had had a maximum effort on tonight's target – 16 aircraft. Theoretically, if we had all arrived back closely bunched together, the last seven aircraft would be circling above oxygen height – up to 15,000ft. Of course, it never quite happened like that, since the spacing of returning aircraft was never that close, nearly always being spread over a reasonable period of time. The highest that we had ever been in the landing pattern was 8,000ft.

From the airfield below two searchlights were pointing upwards, meeting in a cone over the landing area, several thousand feet above us. On one occasion it had been very disconcerting when we had heard a warning from Group that Bandits were about and all of the airfield lighting was switched off. The alarm proved to have been false, and after circling in the darkness for five minutes, and looking in vain for night fighters, the lights came on again and all was well. I watched K King come in for a landing. He made a long low approach, touched down, bounced once slightly, and then rolled smoothly along the runway, gradually slowing down and then turning off at the intersection.

Flying Control came on the air again – "Offstrike to W Willie, Offstrike to W Willie, prepare to land, prepare to land, over". Emmie replied – "W Willie Offstrike, W Willie Offstrike, preparing to land, preparing to land, over". The roar from the propellers changed to a higher key as the pitch on the blades was altered. We were turning into the downwind leg. R/T again "W Willie downwind, over". The propellers increased their whine and the wheels were lowered. Once again Willie shuddered and seemed to halt in mid air. Down came the flaps giving us a feeling of buoyancy, and slowing down our speed further. We swung right round and headed directly into the funnel. R/T again – "W Willie funnel, funnel". The funnel and cross bar lights were rushing up to meet us. Harry was calling out the speed to Emmie. "110, 110, 110, 110, 100, 100, 100, 95, 95, 95, 95, 90, 90, 90, 90". A grey blur flashed by beneath us as we crossed the first section of tarmac. The runway lights tore by on our beams. Willie seemed almost to halt, swooped a little and then glided and the tail commenced to drop. A swishing, then a screech from the tyres as they touched down. One very slight bounce, then the aircraft continued to roll smoothly, though with an occasional very slight bump as we crossed the seams in the concrete, slowing down all the time.

I loosened my clothing, put the guns on "safe", then opened the turret doors and relaxed. Emmie gave the brakes a slight touch. We slowed down rapidly and turned off at the intersection, away from the main runway. I was watching the next aircraft coming in to land. It drifted quite a long way down the runway before touching down, but the landing was smooth. Unfortunately the rear gunner suffered! The tail wheel of the Lancaster is directly underneath the rear turret and occasionally, for no reason that I have ever heard, this wheel developed a "shim" on landing.

Chapter 10 - Munich

When this happened, which was only on rare occasions, the unfortunate rear gunner was shaken about like a pea in a pod. If the pilot braked the aircraft really hard the shaking immediately stopped, failing which it stopped of its own accord when the speed of the aircraft dropped down fairly low. I had suffered from this shaking once or twice on landing, as had all rear gunners, so it wasn't a fault in one machine but apparently an inherent design fault in the construction of the tail wheel assembly. A very minor fault in view of the total excellence of the Lancaster aircraft. We moved slowly around the perimeter track, passing the crew bus that was waiting at an intersection for us to go by before completing the journey with the two crews that had landed ahead of us. It would take them to the Parachute Section first, then on to de-briefing. At last we reached our parking bay. Fred was standing in the entrance, giving us the thumbs up, and directing us onto the parking apron. When we were safely there, Emmie held the brakes on one wheel, and blipped the throttles on the opposite engines, swinging Willie round and facing the exit, ready for our next trip. All the engines were given a final rev, and then shut down. After 8½ hours the silence was deafening!

A return from an operation to Berlin and a dawn landing.

I loosened the straps and hauled myself out of the turret, then crawled on my hands and knees back to the exit hatch. I was first out with my arms full of parachute and sundry other gear. The ground crew were waiting by the exit and Robbie gave me a hand down. I dropped everything and fumbled in my pockets for cigarettes and lighter at the same time trying to answer all Robbie's questions about the trip. The first puff on the cigarette was marvellous, after which I hurriedly moved away and attended to the very urgent needs of nature.

The rest of the crew were clambering along the fuselage towards the rear exit and in a short while waiting for the crew bus to pick us up on his next round. Harry was standing at the front of the aircraft with his torch, and it was then that he discovered that the cannon shell that had gone through the nose had previously passed through the port inner engine cowling. The small flak hole by the Master Compass was also noted.

The headlights of the crew bus were coming round the perimeter track, and we all gave the driver a mighty shout to attract his attention with Nobby flashing his torch to make sure that we had been seen. The driver saw us, turned off, and drove into the dispersal. The bus was empty and we spread ourselves out, taking advantage of this brief rest. A few minutes later we pulled up at the Crew Room adjacent to the parachute section. Dumping our parachutes, Mae Wests and harness onto the counter, we collected our locker keys and very quickly undressed and stowed our flying clothing therein. Red and I were a bit behind the others, having so much to take off, but eventually we were back on the bus for the short journey to the Briefing Room.

We arrived, and inside it was bright and cheerful. The arrangements of the tables and chairs were now different from the original briefing. Each section now had its own table, and we moved around the room as one aircrew, stopping at each table in turn and supplying the interrogating officer with the information applicable to his section.

The first, and most popular table in the room, contained urns of hot coffee and for those who had a taste for it, a tot of really special rum was added. Each member of aircrew was entitled to a ration of the spirit though I seldom touched it myself. To my taste, the rum spoiled the coffee, and the coffee spoiled the rum! Sometimes for a change, I took the rum on its own, before drinking the coffee, though very rarely because from past experience I knew that it would make the effort of keeping awake even more difficult than it already was. On one of my earlier trips I had imbibed a tot added to my coffee and had actually dozed off

Chapter 10 - Munich

while waiting at one of the tables for interrogation. On each of the tables there was a free issue of cigarettes and sweets, both donated by charitable organisations.

We returned our purses, first aid kits and escape aids to one of the NCOs on duty, collecting from him our personal belongings, and then, having obtained our coffee, went to the first table to commence our debrief. At this table the CO was in attendance. Emmie supplied most of the information that was required here, with some help from Ernie and Frank. Main items were time of bombing, our estimation of the success or otherwise of the bombing attack, how we bombed and a host of other details. The two crews who had landed ahead of us were half way through the interrogation, being spread out among the tables ahead of us. The crew that had followed us in were now collecting their coffee and awaiting their turn with the CO.

I looked at the crew board to see if everybody was back. There was a blank against the name of one crew. The Captain was F/O...... We knew this crew well. They had arrived on the squadron soon after us. As soon as we were at the Intelligence Officer's table he would be able to give us the latest news, if any. In the meantime, this one blank spot didn't look too good. By now all the crews should have been back, or at least be in radio contact with base.

The CO finished noting our information and we moved onto the next table occupied by the Intelligence Officer. Here we supplied many more details and information, with each of us contributing something, all helping him to build up a picture with our fragments of the story. When he had finished with us we enquired about the missing crew. They had been officially posted as missing, and there had been no news of them at all. No radio calls had been received, nor "Mayday"(distress call) which could have been attributed to them, nor had the squadron been informed of them landing or crashing, elsewhere. It had therefore to be assumed that they had been shot down. We all felt very sad at this news. We had been good friends with the crew, and in particular I had been very close to their rear gunner, a Scot. We had been together ever since joining the Royal Air Force, sharing the same room at Air Crew Reception Centre at Regents Park. We had completed all our training together, sharing many a jug of beer at local pubs all round England.

We moved on to the next table and the next, until finally, we reached the Gunnery Leaders Section. In response to his usual humorous crack "How many did you get tonight?", we shook him with our answer; "Yes, several contacts and two combats, one lengthy. We jointly claim a JU88 almost certainly destroyed". Recovering quickly, he congratulated us and hurriedly reached out for his pad of Combat Report forms. These were pro-formas to be completed by the gunners concerned after which they would be forwarded to Group for analysis. These reports were examined at length, and on occasions resulted in amended instructions for combat manoeuvres afterwards being forwarded to Squadron Gunnery Leaders for action, these amendments being passed onto the gunners themselves. The forms that we had now completed were very comprehensive, and the many and varied questions asked covered every aspect of the battle.

A few more calls at the Met, Engineering and Camera tables, and we had finished the debriefing. For a few minutes we chatted at the doors with one of the late arrivals. They had seen plenty of "chop" on the trip but had been lucky themselves, not having encountered any fighters. They had only been troubled by the odd flak burst, none of which had been too near. That was the way it often happened. On some trips we had a thoroughly uneventful time, having seen or experienced nothing to be alarmed about, while the next crew to come in returned mainly with the aid of prayers and with large chunks of fuselage missing.

We went outside and clambered onto the crew bus and headed back to the Mess. It was cold in the back of the bus now that we wore only our ordinary attire, but the journey was short and we were soon dismounting at the Mess entrance. We dashed into the wash room to get rid of the worst of the grime from our trip and then hurried into the dining room. The sight of those plates of eggs and bacon was almost more than I could bear! My tongue was hanging out and my mouth watering at this wonderful sight. We each collected our plates, this time complete with baked beans, and sat down at a table where pots of tea were already waiting together with lashings of toast and marmalade.

All around us crews were shooting horrible lines about their exploits and experiences of tonight's operation. As soon as we had got outside of the feast in front of us, we too would lean back, light cigarettes, and shoot a line with the best of them. After all, we'd had two combats with JU88s as well as being Aunt Sally for several near misses. Another crew arrived and sat down at our table. They too had met with opposition in the target area becoming involved with an ME110. A running battle had taken place, with both aircraft eventually breaking off the encounter with no apparent damage on either side.

After we had finished eating we went into the bar and got some beer,

Chapter 10 - Munich

after which we found some comfortable chairs in the ante room. It was only then that I learned of an additional hazard that we had undergone during our journey back, soon after our last combat. Ernie told us that at the time only he and Frank were aware of the problem. They decided to keep it to themselves for the time being since it would only add to the strains that we were all suffering without serving any useful purpose.

What had happened was that on the return journey, and prior to recrossing the German border on the way home, the Germans had successfully interfered with Gee, which in any case would have been at extreme range. Astro Navigation was impossible since the greater part of the journey back over Germany and France was done with cloud above and below us. The Nav team had already tried H_2S, but the screen was full of mush and was no help. The only form of navigation left was dead reckoning – very difficult under the present conditions. Not being aware of the problems, Emmie kept asking for a position report, and they were sweating to comply without really being able to do so, and were not too happy trying to appear more confident than they really were!

Despite an occasional glimpse of the ground through chinks in the clouds, they were still lost. Eventually ETA (estimated time of arrival) the French coast had come and gone for some considerable time matters were not improved. Finally the cloud thinned, and through the gap the French coast could be seen dimly, although our exact position was still uncertain. Frank tried the H_2S again, and through the mush was just able to distinguish a part of the coast by Boulogne that ran almost due north/south – the only piece of coast like it! We were then only three miles to starboard of track. At this time, as Frank said, he called up on to the intercom and said "I have a fix", to which one of us cheeky buggers down at the back said "This will be good" – and it was!

Although our route back was almost a straight run from Lake Geneva to the French coast, one of the causes of the trouble and delay was a jet stream which unknown to us was blowing down our track – a 50 knot head wind. Thus, there was no drift, but our ETA was considerably delayed. I asked Ernie why he had been so confident when I had asked him what the river was during one of the brief clear periods. He said the Seine was the only river on our port side on the return route which would have been big enough for me to see.

A big sing-song had started up in the bar but we decided, on this occasion, that bed was more alluring, and decided to go back to the billet. Our bicycles were waiting where we had left them outside the Mess, and

View from a Birdcage

off we cycled into the darkness. It was cold, very quiet, and the air was lovely after the smoky Mess. In another hour the birds would be around with their pre-dawn chorus. The searchlights over the airfield had been switched off which meant that all of the aircraft in Bomber Command had now landed. Although this light had gone, we were very familiar with the roads and paths on our camp and had no difficulty finding our way back. When we got in the fire was still glowing. We had banked it up before leaving and the room was warm and cosy. On top of the stove we had left a full kettle of water and a small plume of steam was issuing from the spout. In spite of our tiredness, we decided to have just one cup of cocoa each. Frank got busy with the cups and condensed milk while I wrote a brief note to our batman which I pinned on the outside of the door – "Please do not wake any of us before midday".

We sat round the fire drinking our cocoa and enjoying the peace and quiet, and then, in unison, we washed up and put away the cups and commenced to undress. Slowly I wriggled out of my flying underclothing, then put on pyjamas and got into an incredibly appealing bed. I lay there for a few minutes in silent and contented luxury. Thoughts went through my mind in quick succession... wonder if we shall be off next Saturday?... Must change my gauntlets tomorrow, the zips broken... Emmie had a good landing tonight...

Someone turned off the light. I said my small prayer and then opened my eyes. There was a comforting glow on the ceiling, reflections from the fire. In the next bed to me Ernie muttered "Good night". I tried to reply but the words didn't come. I was just verging on that edge of nothingness that comes before sleep. In the roof there was a fluttering as the early birds wakened. A coal dropped out of the fire into the grate. Somewhere a fox was barking, but at last even listening was too much of an effort...I slept.

CHAPTER 11
PRESS ON REGARDLESS

Memories of the Munich trip faded as we continued taking part in the process of battering Germany. Operation followed operation; – Merseburg, Zeitz, Gelsenkirchen, Mainz, Cleve, Politz, Dresden, Chemnitz, Kassel, Essen, Wuppertal, Bottrop, Osnabruck, Kiel, Potsdam...we never seemed to rest. During the more recent weeks the Royal Air Force had been concentrating on the bombing of synthetic oil installations with occasional tactical targets to aid the Allied ground forces who by now were well established on the continent of Europe and close to the German border. During these missions we had experienced our fair share of fighter attacks and flak damage, but still luck remained with us, and although the mental scarring continued, we were still in good heart and operating efficiently. Old friends and crews ceased to fly with us, some successfully completing their tours though sadly others were never to do so.

The crew prior to take off on a 'daylight'. Seated (back) l to r; Red, myself. Standing, l to r, Harry, Frank, Emmie, Jack and Ernie.

View from a Birdcage

My log book entry for February 1945 including the entry of 13th February for the Dresden raid.

A typical page of my log book. This example cover May 1944 and details the date and time of take off of the raid, the aircraft used, the pilot, my duty on board, remarks and the flying time recorded.

Chapter 11 - Press on Regardless

Eventually we completed our second tour and we now had 60 operations behind us. At the end of our first tour of 30 operations we decided to carry on with tour No 2, and after a brief but hectic leave period we were back, refreshed in mind, body and spirit, ready for whatever was to come. As of now we had decided to carry on with our third tour, ready for whatever was to come, but supremely confident.

Of those post Munich trips, several had made their marks on us and were never to be forgotten. Included on these was the operation on Dresden. This raid was the subject of numerous stories in the post-war years. It seemed to me that some, at least, of these stories were politically motivated, though I have no personal comments to pass on the feelings so engendered. As far as we, and all the other aircrews were concerned, we never queried the morality of any raid; our target was a precision engineering works a not unusual aiming point. The distance from base to target was quite considerable, and it would be the deepest penetration into Germany that we had so far made, though the time taken while long would not be our longest trip. It was in the south east corner of the country, very close to the Polish and Czech borders. At briefing we learned that it was a maximum effort, involving 800 Lancasters and Halifaxes. The attack was to be in two waves, 400 aircraft on target at 2200 hours and the other 400 aircraft at 2400 hours. We were on the second attack. Fortunately, at this stage of the war the German fighter defences had tailed off, with the bulk of their fighter defences operating on their western borders against the Allied invasion. It was for this reason that our route to Dresden was less tortuous than it would have been in the past. The journey nonetheless was very tiring, taking over eight hours to complete. Take off was 2150 and after briefing we were able to enjoy our usual game of pontoon at the dispersal.

By 2215 we were out over the North Sea and approaching our operational height of 20,000ft. The weather was pretty clear, and although cold was bearable. Crossing the coast of north Holland we were subjected to an ack ack barrage of medium intensity, though experiencing no near misses. There was a suggestion of some fighter activity in the distance though we were not involved, nor did we see any action in the form of combats. By now, we were over northern Germany, and having five minutes in hand, Emmie decided to do a dog leg, turning off to port. Just before we turned back on course, I saw to the south east, a distant glare in the sky. I mentioned this over the intercom and Ernie took a bearing. Back came the reply, "Dresden lies along that line". We were at this time several hundred miles away from Dresden and Ernie continued to navigate in the normal manner. Emmie kept an eye on the glow and it never deviated from our course, continuing to brighten as we neared the source of the light. Eventually it dawned upon us that it was the glow from our target, and was the result of the attack by the earlier force on target at 2200 hours.

When eventually we started our bombing run, I saw a conflagration which must have equalled the fire storms started by the raids on Hamburg earlier in the war. By the time that we reached the target all the ack ack batteries had been swamped and silenced and we didn't see one burst of shell fire, nor any fighter opposition. We dropped our markers and bombs and headed home. Apart from minor isolated flak, we had a good run back to England. At debrief, fatigue caught up with me and I fell quietly asleep until being rudely awakened by a nudge from Harry. We tumbled into our beds around 6 am and slept like logs until wakened for lunch.

Exactly a month after the raid on Dresden, we were engaged in an operation which was quite an adventure, and most unusual for us. Our Squadron Commander at this time was Wing Commander "Tubby" Baker, a most likeable character and a very experienced pilot, who was popular with us all. Squadron Commanders were appointed on the recommendation of Group, and one of the normal requirements was that the appointment be made to a pilot with a long record of successful operations. The work undertaken by Squadron Commanders took up all their time, and because they were involved almost totally with their aircrews, and with the Station Commander, they had little time available for flying on operations. They were however allowed to fly on an occasional bombing raid, thus maintaining their flying status and pay. On one such occasion we were to benefit.

Tubby decided that the time was ripe for him to do another operational raid. His record of operations at this time was quite outstanding. He had been a bomber pilot since early in the war, and had always done his operations on what were then known as "heavies". That is multiple engined aircraft such as Whitleys, Blenheims and Wellingtons, eventually graduating to Lancasters and Halifaxes when these aircraft became available towards mid-war. At the present time his score stood at 99 operations. To our great surprise, on this one, his hundredth, we were honoured to supply our aircraft Willie to be largely crewed by us on what was almost an historical occasion.

This would be the first trip that we would do without Emmie as our

Chapter 11 - Press on Regardless

pilot. It would be a strange feeling, though after Emmie, Tubby would have been my choice. On this trip he was taking as his crew our own Nav team, Ernie and Frank, and Red and myself as his air gunners. He would be taking his own Wireless Operator and Flight Engineer who were respectively the Squadron Engineering and Signals leaders.

The next day the trip was laid on, and we knew by the briefing time that it was to be a daylight operation. We were now into March and the weather looked hopeful, being a bright mild day. Briefing was at midday and after the usual flying meal in the Mess, we arrived at the Briefing Room. When the curtains were drawn we saw that it was a new target for us – Wuppertal, a manufacturing complex in the heart of the Ruhr. We also saw that our additional duty was to be Master Bomber – quite a trip it promised to be! Take off was at 1315, and as always we were out at the dispersal in good time. After the checks had been completed on Willie, we decided to forego our usual game of cards and instead we played cricket with a tennis ball and a batten of scrap wood.

Fifteen minutes before take off the CO dropped in on us for his usual chat, and immediately after he left us we climbed aboard Willie and slowly taxied out of the dispersal and onto the perimeter track. There were twelve of our squadron's aircraft on this raid, and we led the way to the marshalling point. We lined up on 24 runway and after a brief spell running up we got the green from the caravan, and we were on our way. This time we exited the UK at Orford Ness. It was still fine and sunny when we reached operational height and the temperature was only 18 degrees below zero, relatively mild for operations, and with all my flying clothing and heating on I remained warm and comfortable. Crossing the coast of Belgium we received the usual greeting from the flak batteries, though none were too close at hand.

Looking back I could see the main force in the distance – 250 heavies. We had only been over enemy territory for a short while when I saw a small gaggle of Mossies about 5,000ft above us, and rapidly catching up. We knew from the earlier briefing that this small force were doing a spoof raid on another target about 80 miles from where we were to bomb. I doubt that they were able to see me as they passed over, but I waved them good luck just in case. We droned steadily on until we were within 30 miles of the target, when Tubby came on the intercom to tell us that there was a very heavy flak barrage over Wuppertal. In a few minutes we were in the thick of it. All the flak was predicted, and uncomfortably close and accurate – the fine clear weather saw to that. We were approaching

A Lancaster just aft and below us. Taken from my turret on the way to Wuppertal.

On the way to Wuppertal a Lancaster travelling on our port quarter. Taken from my turret.

the bombing run and I locked my turret in readiness. A minute later I heard Frank say "Bomb doors open", and very soon afterwards "Bombs gone". It wasn't often that I was able to see our bombs and markers going down, but with the bright sun prevailing I watched them dropping for several thousand feet before they were lost in the industrial haze. Shortly afterwards I saw our red and green markers burst on the ground and the explosions from the accompanying bombs. By now our photos had been taken and the bomb doors closed. Close behind other Pathfinders were dropping their markers, and main force commenced bombing. We climbed about 3,000ft above all the other aircraft, circled the target, and watched how the raid was progressing.

Chapter 11 - Press on Regardless

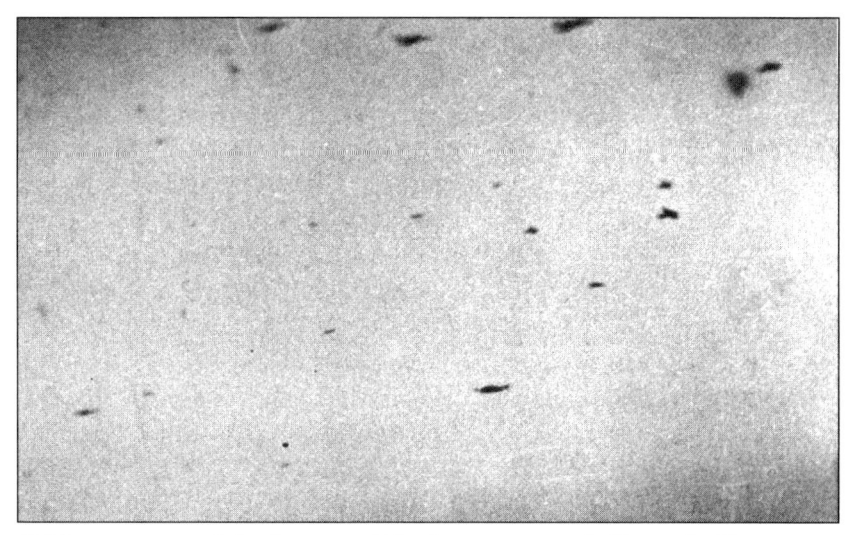

Flak bursts amongst main bomber stream. Taken from my turret on the Wuppertal raid.

For a while, all went well, but gradually "bomb creep" began to take place, and some aircraft were bombing early. Nobby switched on the radio transmitter and Tubby broadcast in plain language to the deputy Master Bomber. He instructed him to re-mark the aiming point with a yellow sky marker, for by now there was too much smoke to see the ground clearly. Down went the marker, and it burst at about 3,000ft, with golden rain dropping. The subsequent effect was immediately noticeable, and once again, the main force bombs were falling bang on target. Amazingly the flak continued unabated and we saw two Lancs hit. One had his starboard inner engine on fire, and was turning for home, losing height only very slowly. I think that he had already dropped his bombs and provided that he remained unmolested, and if they were able to feather the engine and put out the fire, they should have reached their base safely. The other Lanc was grievously damaged. I could see that one fin and rudder had been shot away and very little of the rear turret remained. They stood no chance at all and they plummeted out of the sky with none of the aircrew getting out. It eventually exploded on the ground on the outskirts of Wuppertal. I said a prayer for them and advised Ernie of the details for logging.

By now the bombing was over and we circled the target once more while Tubby assessed, as best he could, the result of the raid, after which we set a new course for home. We gradually began losing height, and I was thinking how lucky we had been when, without any warning we ran into a vicious predicted flak barrage from the outer suburbs of Wuppertal. By now, we were all on our own, the rest of the bombers being 8 or 10 miles ahead of us and well away from any flak. One lone Lanc was a gift to the German gun predictors, and despite immediate evasive action, we had two or three very near misses. The fumes from the explosive assailed my sense of smell, and I could hear a lot of shell fragments hitting the aircraft. Later we were to see that Willie had been peppered but without any vital damage being caused. I also discovered that there was a ¼inch score in the Perspex on the port side of my turret. This must have been caused by a jagged shell fragment only inches away from where I sat. After what seemed an age, but in reality was only a few minutes, we left the barrage behind and settled down to flying straight and level. One of the advantages of flying on daylight operations was that the never ending weaving that we did on night flying operations was unnecessary. In the conditions under which we were now flying we could see clearly for several miles in all directions, and were thus unlikely to suffer a surprise attack.

We were just about half way to the Channel coast when I noticed a small black speck just below and behind us on the starboard quarter. It was obviously an aircraft but without knowing exactly what type it was, it was impossible to judge its distance from us. The black speck was very rapidly increasing in size, so I switched on the intercom and said "Fighter attack developing from starboard down quarter – dive starboard- GO". We took a sickening dive down to starboard and commenced a very steep weave. As soon as we began these evasive manoeuvres, the fighter which I now knew that it was, disappeared starboard up at an amazing speed, but not before I was astounded to recognize it as a Messerschmitt 163. This was the first German rocket fighter to come into operational service, and for nearly a year we had had its silhouette on our aircraft recognition screens.

When he passed us he was at least a half a mile away from where we were and posed no immediate threat. His lack of success in the attack was due to the very high attacking speed, at least 100 mph faster than conventional propeller driven German fighters. Because of this very high speed, the turning circle was immensely greater than that of the comparatively lumbering Lancaster. Thus, we were able to turn way inside of him, depriving the pilot of a target at which to aim. The normal enemy fighter was more able to match the speed of its potential victim, and perhaps score a point blank shot. We straightened out of the weave

Chapter 11 - Press on Regardless

and saw the fighter way out on the beam, and by now at least three miles away. The pilot made one more half hearted attack on us with even less success than on the first occasion. Unfortunately, at no time was the fighter near enough to Willie for us to get off any shots at him. Another basic fault with this type of propulsion was that it had very limited range. The total flying time available was no more than about 30 minutes. At this stage the rocket fuel was exhausted, and the fighter had to glide back to its base and land on skids. On take off it had wheels, but for design reasons it was unable to retain these for landing. The wheels were automatically discarded immediately after take off.

Once more we had settled down to quiet level flying. We crossed the coast with no flak barrage, and some four hours after take off we landed back at Downham Market. When we piled out of the aircraft onto the dispersal we were horrified to see the large number of shell splinter holes. Fortunately for us they were all comparatively small, the damage being mainly cosmetic. We did subsequently discover that a shell splinter had passed through both sides of the "Elsan" – yet another reason for waiting patiently until we had landed!

A small convoy of vehicles approached us, the CO's car in the lead. When they arrived out piled a motley throng of individuals, including photographers from the station Photo Section. Even more welcome was a crate of beer off loaded from one of the vans. Tubby was toasted by us all on the completion of his 100th operation. There was taken, one particularly good picture of us all standing by "Willie" (Years later it was reproduced in 'Lancaster at War'). Back at de-brief we were the centre of attention, particularly when it became known that we had been attacked by a Messerschmitt 163. It had been seen by several other aircraft engaged on the raid, but we were the only aircraft to have been attacked by the rocket plane, half hearted though it was. I believe that the attack may have been made on us because we were "tail end Charlie" some miles behind the rest of the main stream.

As we drove away in the crew bus heading for the Mess and the flying meal, my mind went back to a very strange incident that I had experienced after an operation a few weeks before. On this occasion we had returned and finished our de-brief at about the same time as tonight. On that particular day I had ridden down to the briefing room on my bicycle so when we came out after de-brief the rest of the crew climbed on to the bus and headed for the Mess, and I walked over to the crew room to pick up my bike, eventually leaving for the Mess about 15 minutes after the crew.

163

View from a Birdcage

The photo taken on return from the raid on Wuppertal, 12/3/45. The celebrations are for the pilot's 100th operation. From left to right: F/O Jack Catford, rear gunner, Flt Lt Ernie Mawson, Navigator, Flt Lt Frank Jackson, B/Aimer, Flt Lt Ben Bennett, W/Operator, Wg Cdr "Tubby" Baker, Pilot, Flt Lt Ron Flatt, Engineer, Flt Lt "Red" Winch, M/U Gunner, S/Ldr Gordon Hawes, B/Aimer II.

In fact I quite enjoyed the seven or eight minutes exercise riding along in the cool fresh air. In due course I arrived at a very dark and quiet mess. The darkness was quite usual, with all the blackout curtains in place, but what had happened to the normal hum of conversation punctuated by boisterous laughter from the bar? The normal sing song was also conspicuous by its absence; it was normally a feature of an operation successfully completed.

Propping my bike up in the cycle rack I went through the light lock and into the vestibule. All the lights were on, but no cheerful little WAAF to greet me. I went into the ante room. A big fire was burning, with all the lights on. Books papers, and magazines were strewn around, and even a few cigarettes were burning themselves out in the ash trays. By now I was convinced that I was experiencing a land lubber's "Marie Celeste"! A quick visit to the bar disclosed no bodies, just partially consumed drinks with a few cigarettes burning away. A similar state of affairs was found in the dining room – no signs of life, only half consumed meals littered around. By now I was almost convinced that I was suffering from post operational hysteria and I beat a hurried retreat outside.

Once in the open I waited for a few moments for my eyes to become

Chapter 11 - Press on Regardless

acclimatised to the darkness and was about to get on my bike and beat a hurried retreat to the billet, when I noticed 20 yards or so up the road leading to the main entrance to the Mess two cigarettes glowing in the dark. I walked up and from out of the darkness two SPs appeared, obviously on duty. Their amazement at seeing me was even greater than mine at seeing them. Happily for me my peace of mind was restored by what they told me.

Just after we had landed from tonight's operation six Mosquitos from 608 Squadron, who shared the station with us, had taken off for a late nuisance raid on the Third Reich. Unfortunately one of the Mossies had an engine failure just after becoming airborne and had crash landed in the field behind the Officers' Mess. Fortunately the pilot and navigator walked away from the aircraft more or less unhurt, but his bomb load comprising of one cookie (4,000lb) had not gone off. As had already been mentioned, these bombs were very unstable and it was decided to evacuate the Mess until daylight when the armament boys could commence the highly dangerous job of nullifying the bomb. Happily they were successful in accomplishing this.

The SPs hadn't realised that one member of aircrew was returning by bicycle and coming in via the back entrance to the Mess, hence the comedy of errors. I was pleased to know that I should be able to join up with the rest of my crew at the Sergeants' Mess where extra meals had hurriedly been laid on. This Mess was quite some distance from the crashed Mossie.

During the course of our second tour we had been engaged on three operations that involved tactical support for the British Army and the Allied Forces. One was at Cleve, just across the Rhine. Field Marshal Montgomery's forces had been blocked in their attempt at crossing the Rhine because of a massive build up of German armour and troops in this town. A raid was laid on with many hundreds of bombers being engaged. The trip for us was uneventful but satisfying in as much as we knew that the town had been evacuated of its civilian occupants and contained only German Army personnel and their armour. The number of aircraft used on this small target was rather akin to cracking the proverbial nut with a sledge hammer, but tactically it was essential to neutralise and take out the town. Of the raid itself, all we could see was a carpet of fire. Some weeks later photographs that had been taken of this target by reconnaissance aircraft on the day following the raid were shown to the Squadron. These depicted an area of wasteland, not dissimilar to photographs taken in the

View from a Birdcage

trench areas on the Western Front during World War One. All that was left of Cleve was an enormous pile of rubbish with nothing even faintly resembling a house or building of any kind. Shortly after this raid, the Army successfully crossed the Rhine by-passing the shattered town.

Wesel, on the Rhine and near to Cleve. This photo gives an idea of the devastation caused by our attack. Denuding the German defences allowed Monty's army to cross the river.

We did another Army co-op on Boxing Day, 26th December 1944. The Squadron had a stand down on Christmas Day, so we were not displeased that we had some action on the next day. The operation was to be another daylight trip and the weather was perfect – brilliant sunshine and no cloud, though the temperature even on the ground was well below freezing point. This suggested a most uncomfortable trip so far as I was concerned. I shuddered to think what the temperature would be at 20,000ft. Briefing was at 1130, and we were fascinated to learn of our task. The target was St Vith in the Ardennes area. Following the German breakthrough in this region, fighting had been intense for some time, and it was only now that the Allies were commencing to counter attack.

The raid was to be heavy and its purpose was to destroy German armour and their troops on the front line. The big problem was that the Allied and German armies were very close together in what was described as a fluid situation. Under such conditions there would inevitably be grave risk, or some at least, of the Allied armies being subjected to our bombing attack. This was an unacceptable risk to Bomber Command so with accurate battle front grid references, the Pathfinders were to be used in an operation code-named "Long Stop". We were all to carry canisters of brown smoke bombs, and our task was to clearly mark a safety line beyond which the Royal Air Force bombers could drop their high explosives without putting at risk the lives of Allied Forces.

Take off time was at 1220, and at this time we were duly airborne and setting course for the north coast of France. Apart from the cold, which was intense, even in daylight, flying conditions were perfect. At this stage in the war the Luftwaffe fighters were being used largely for tactical purposes. Consequently it was believed that we should not be troubled by them - which in fact proved to be the case. We forged steadily ahead with a large force of bombers clearly visible behind us.

We crossed the coast on the French/Belgian borders and within about 15 minutes were due on the bombing run. Harry called out that there was flak ahead of us, and within a few minutes we were in the thick of it. By now we were over the battle front and could clearly see the artillery on both sides pooping away at each other. The predicted flak was less accurate than usual and, apart from two fairly near misses, caused us little trouble. There was one Halifax behind which seemed to be in some kind of trouble, and in due course he turned away towards home. The bombing run commenced and I locked my turret and waited. "Bomb doors open" said Frank, and shortly afterwards, "Bombs gone". The bomb doors closed, and I looked below as I unlocked my turret. I saw a massive wall of thick brown smoke rising to several thousand feet in the still clear air. By now the high explosive was pouring down, well beyond the smoke barrier in the woods and open country below. Thankfully I didn't see one explosion on the wrong side of the smoke screen, and we heard afterwards that the raid had achieved its purpose.

The first half of the journey home was uneventful, but when we crossed the English coast thick fog commenced to build up on the ground and it became more dense by the minute. When we were within minutes of landing instructions came over the radio that the fog was dense at Downham Market and landing was out of the question. We were diverted to RAF Gravely, some 50 miles from Downham. We were amazed at these instructions since our own airfield was equipped with "Fido", a very useful landing aid under the prevailing conditions, and one we had used successfully on many other occasions when we had experienced dense fog. Why we were not using it that day was a mystery. We duly diverted and landed without incident at Gravely, which was still in the clear, and in fact enjoying sunshine. After de-brief we spent a miserable night in Nissen huts miles from anywhere. To add to our misery, fuel for stoves was very short at this time, so trying to sleep was not a very happy experience. We had an early breakfast, and as the fog over East Anglia had lifted, we took off and were back at Downham Market by 0830.

Diversions such as we had just experienced were welcome in an emergency but were rarely enjoyed. There was always the feeling of being waifs and strays, and although our hosts always did their best, they were faced with a very difficult problem in having, very suddenly and with little warning, to have to billet anything up to an extra 100 bodies. Thus one had to put up with very cramped and sometimes primitive conditions and scrappy meals. On one such occasion, earlier in the war we had a similar diversion to Ford on the Sussex coast. When we arose the following morning, after a miserable nights sleep, the airfield was an amazing sight. Practically every Allied war plane was represented, and there must have been at least twenty different types of aircraft parked on the airfield. They were parked in every possible place. Flying control had done a marvellous job in getting them all safely down and away from the runways.

CHAPTER 12
WAR'S END

May 1945 arrived. Holland had just been liberated and it seemed that at long last, the war was coming to an end, or at least ending in Europe. On May 3rd operations were laid on with an early briefing at 0930. Then we settled down in the Briefing Room, we found that our trip was to be a most joyous event. The target was Rotterdam and our bomb bays were to be filled with tins and packages of food. Throughout the war the Dutch people, and particularly the town dwellers, had existed on a near starvation diet, which as the Allies progressed towards victory became less and less. During the weeks before the collapse of German resistance in Holland, food supplies had diminished almost to vanishing point. An SOS from the Dutch resistance brought the seriousness of the situation to the notice of the Allied High Command - hence this hurriedly arranged trip. The official code name of the mission was "Operation Manna", but before we had left the Briefing Room, the aircrew had already re-christened it "Operation Spam". Take off was 1115 and time on target 1155. The food was to be dropped in the middle of Rotterdam airport, and the Dutch authorities had promised to mark the aiming point with a huge white cross.

When we arrived at the dispersal, the last of the food was being stowed away in Willie's bomb bays. The tins and packages were placed in panniers that were hooked onto the bomb release mechanism. What a happy sight it was! Never before had we been so content with our cargo. The day was fine and we were airborne by 1115 and set course for the East Anglia coast, a few minutes flying time away. We were at 1,000 feet, but quickly came down to 500 feet and thoroughly enjoyed what to us was hedge hopping. The sense of speed was exhilarating, almost unknown to us before except on take off. It seemed that only a few minutes had passed before Emmie came on to the intercom and said "Dutch coast ahead". With the Skipper's permission, I locked the turret and scrambled along and up into the Pilot's compartment. We quickly crossed the beaches, which surprisingly were very crowded with the local population. News of our errand must have spread like wild fire. They waved frantically to us as we passed over. I got back into my turret and as soon as we had left the coast we climbed to 2,000 feet within a few minutes we had reached Rotterdam Airport. There, slap in the middle, was the white cross that had been promised for our use as the aiming point. Before opening the bomb doors we made one circuit of the airfield. The airport and approach roads were black with people madly waving to us with Dutch and British flags. They must have secretly hoarded these for over five years. We settled down on to the "bombing run". Soon I heard the bomb doors opening, and shortly afterwards the food was released. I had a wonderful view of the cross as we flew over, and saw the food parcels still falling onto the cross. I managed to get a quick photograph from my turret, and chucked out a packet of 20 Players as my personal contribution. The journey home took barely 50 minutes and was again done at low level, whilst we were over the sea. We all agreed that this had been a wonderful "bombing" trip – would that they had all been

Operation Manna (we called it the Spam raid), Rotterdam 3/5/45. The war was not yet quite over but attention was turning to the plight of the inhabitants of formerly occupied Europe. The cross on the centre of the airfield is the aiming point. Lancs bombed this aiming point with hundreds of tons of tinned food for the starving population. The specks all over the field are the food bundles.

like this one.

Following the trip to Rotterdam it seemed incredible to us that operations were over. "No more dicing with death" – a popular phrase amongst aircrew. During the next few weeks we got in an amazing amount of flying, and a variety of odd jobs and duties that Air Ministry found for us. We flew 10 airmen on posting to Brussels and on the return journey bought back 24 British ex prisoners of war. What a joyous trip that was! The old Lancaster had no comforts to offer passengers, but they cared not, for this was the trip that they had dreamed of for many a long weary year. Two of them managed to lie on the rest bed and the rest sat on the hard floor. Emmie allowed each of them in turn to go up into the cockpit, and even a visit to our turrets was much in demand and granted. The return journey was little over an hour, and there were tears in the eyes of most of the soldiers when they saw England below. Many of them had been POWs since Dunquerque. We landed them in Westcott, in Bucks, where the Army took them under their care. We had a quick

Brussels airfield. Awaiting take off with ex-POWs.

cup of NAAFI and took off for Downham Market.

Our next trip was even more interesting. We had a similar job to do, but this time we were to land in Lubeck near the German Baltic coast. We had bombed this town and were interested to see the results, even though the raid had taken place a long time before. In the event however, the Luftwaffe night fighter airfield on which we landed was a long way from the town so we were unable to see it. Our main ambition when we arrived there was to search for Luger pistols or Schmeisser semi-automatic guns. However, search as we did we had no luck. The Tactical Air Force command were there three days ahead of us. They had now moved on, but we guessed that they had scooped the pool where German small arms were concerned. I did manage to bring back with me a German helmet and soldier's (Feldwebels) uniform. The most useful memento of this visit was obtained from a tool kit on a JU88 night fighter – a hammer that

Lubeck 10/5/45. Len in front of a JU88 nightfighter.

Myself and Roy standing by a JU88 wearing German uniforms.

I use to this day.

We stopped overnight in the German Officers' Mess, a real taste of luxury unlike the largely pre-fabricated RAF Officers' Mess. There were lawns going down to a picturesque lake – what a place to live in! During the afternoon of our first day at Lubeck we decided to go for a walk across the local countryside. Because the German troops and Luftwaffe had only left the area a few days before, we had decided before leaving Downham Market to take with us our issue Smith & Wesson .38s. We had rarely worn these on ops since an armed member of aircrew, if he had baled out and become an evader, was in a rather dangerous situation, and if armed could be shot out of hand.

Circumstances were quite different now, and it was comforting to wear my .38. It was eerie walking down the quiet country lanes. We passed a few cottages, in all of which we could feel curious eyes peering at us

Lubeck. Roy & Len in front of the Luftwaffe Officers' Mess.

from behind drawn curtains! In a lane we found a German ammunition truck, which in its haste to escape had been driven into a ditch and lay on its side, quite deserted. We clambered onto it and discovered that it was full of stick grenades. I took a couple with me and when we had moved to a safe distance from the truck, I pulled the tapes and lobbed them over a hedge. It sounded like the start of World War Three! The next day we

Chapter 12 - War's End

took off with another load of ex POWs. This time they were all seamen, mostly Lascars, who had been captured by a German surface raider in the Indian Ocean four years before. The pleasure at their release was heartening to see, and to judge by the look of them, they were even closer

Our load of Lascar ex-POWs at Brussels. They had been captured by a German raider in the Indian Ocean.

Brussels, prior to loading up.

Brussels. Some of the ex-POWs. I am on the left handing out the smokes.

to starvation than their Occidental counterparts.

Following our return, we were saddened to lose Emmie. He had for some time held the rank of Wing Commander, and was now posted, in the rank of Acting Group Captain, to be CO at another station in 8 Group. What followed was even worse! Shortly after his posting, he was taken seriously ill and rushed off to RAF Hospital, Ely for an urgent operation. During the latter part of our missions we knew that he hadn't been well, though he tried to keep this from us and from the Medics on station. At no time was his piloting skill affected, but undoubtedly the strain of his responsibilities made certain of his eventual collapse from a duodenal ulcer which burst. Thankfully he made a good recovery and left the Service.

Our new pilot was a likeable bloke, Flt Lt Johnny Bulling. He was good at his job and fitted in well with us. By now we had lost Ernie and Frank who had been repatriated to New Zealand, so we also had a new Nav team. We all got on well together though flying was now easy work, with no operations to bother about. In fact, with the greatest respect for our new crew members, we should not have been happy at flying on operations without Emmie, Ernie and Frank.

After our trip to Lubeck our next flight was a bit of a highlight. It was code named "Cooks Tour", and was laid on especially to enable us to take our ground crew on a trip. Their hard and faithful work together with all the other ground crews deserved no less. "Cooks Tour" was a low level daylight trip over "Happy Valley" in the Ruhr to show the ground crews the results of the attacks that we had been able to make as a result of their dedicated work in keeping us and our machines flying. Strangely enough, for us and our passengers, this trip proved to be an anti climax. We were

Chapter 12 - War's End

just approaching Duisberg, and were down to 3,000 feet when we had an engine failure! During operations there was no way that a Pathfinder aircrew were permitted to return as a result of a single engine failure. Things were different now, and any engine failure required us to return to base. Sadly we turned back for home, only having had time for a quick look at Duisburg, terribly battered, and now fading into the distance as we slowly climbed away for the return trip.

All ended satisfactorily though, since on our return we were told that the trip would be laid on again the next day. Came the morning and once again we had a fine day and all went well with Willie. Ironically enough, the previous day we had flown in N Nan whilst Willie was undergoing an engine change in the hangars. We flew over Duisberg, then Essen, Munster and Wuppertal. We flew very low and the damage caused by our raids was awe inspiring square mile after square mile of utter devastation and ruins. Our ground crew couldn't believe their eyes, nor for that matter could we. Bombing, as we had, from 20,000 feet, all that we had been able to see was explosions, fire and smoke, the rest being up to our imagination. Now we knew. At last the trip ended and we turned for home. The ground crew were talking about it for days afterwards.

Next we did a couple of trips to Flensburg in Denmark. During the war the Germans had a big radio location station there and the British scientists and the Royal Air Force wanted to evaluate it. These trips proved to be somewhat boring, since on both days we had 10/10ths cloud cover below, and consequently were unable to see anything of Denmark. We did dummy bombing runs on a target below, doing innumerable runs on different bearings. The target was unseen with our eyes, but clearly discernible on the H_2S tube. We were receiving instructions from the scientists below via radio, and commenced each run from about 20 miles out to sea. We saw five other Lancasters engaged on the same duties. The exercise lasted about an hour and a half, and we were pleased when we had the recall signal.

From what we had learned during the war, the German early warning systems were good, but not up to the standards of our equipment until near to the end of the war. Their main advantage was their proximity to the coast of England as a result of their occupation of the whole of Northern Europe, thus enabling them to apply a much longer network of radar defences. We never learned of the results of the exercises on which we had been engaged at Flensburg.

By now we were back into normal routine training, and were doing fairly frequent navigational exercises - but with a difference. Now that the war in Europe was over, these exercises were frequently laid on to include us flying over France, Belgium and Holland. This was a change, and most welcome. There was not nearly so much flying over all the well known routes in the UK. In addition, we occasionally made brief landings on the continent.

In August 1945 we had a real boost to our morale. This was "Operation Dodge", which required Lancasters to be used in a trooping role by flying to Bari on the Adriatic Coast of southern Italy. We were to stay there for two days, and on the morning of the third day bring back British Army personnel on leave. The great day arrived when we were to do our first trip, which was a long one of approx 7 hours. Sadly, poor old Willie had by now completely retired, and aircrew were flying in any available aircraft. We set off in T Tommy and had an enjoyable trip, and quite uneventful. Our route took us right across France. From the Pas des Calais, where we had an excellent view of the buzz bomb sites which we

On the way to Bari- Vesuvius and Naples.

had helped to shatter, and out into the Mediterranean over Marseilles.

From the south coast of France we skirted Corsica and Sardinia and carried on down to Naples where we turned to port, right over Vesuvius and the mountainous country of central southern Italy, arriving at Bari on the opposite coast. Before these trips had commenced we had all been

Chapter 12 - War's End

Landing at Bari, southern Italy. Taken from mid-upper turret.

equipped with tropical clothing and were very pleased with this new outfit because when we arrived at Bari the temperatures were in the high 90s. We had also received boosters for our various inoculations. Following our arrival we were briefed on the details of our stay. Our time was our own until the morning of take-off which was at 0800 hrs. Bari itself was five miles away, but the Royal Air Force ran a frequent bus service to the town and back again so there were no problems in sightseeing. We were given the choice of being billeted on the camp, or making our own arrangements and staying in Bari. The RAF had been successful in requisitioning the best hotel in town, the Imperiale, and on our second trip we sampled the delights offered at this hotel. For 2/6d per night I had a marvellous room with a view over the sea and harbour. There was a bathroom attached, all in marble with a sunken bath tub and a bidet. I felt like Nero – what luxury!

On this, our first trip, we all decided to spend our days in Bari and to return to the camp at night. Off we went to town with its magnificent tree lined boulevards, and shops overflowing with merchandise, largely black market. We decided that swimming was the order of the day, and during the whole of the afternoon we remained submerged in sea water that was almost tepid. Most of the sea front in Bari faced the harbour, and such beaches as there were in the vicinity were scruffy. Our swimming problem had been solved by information supplied by another crew whom we had met in town. We went down to the harbour and hired an Italian boatman who rowed the seven of us out to sea where we had a most delightful afternoon, alternatively diving into the sea and climbing back again. It was so hot by the time that we had clambered back into the boat; we were dry again, so back we plunged into the water! For three hours of this delight, the boatman was overjoyed with his reward 20 Woodbines! It seemed that on the black market he could obtain enough from the sale of the Woodbines to maintain his family for a week. They just weren't interested in Lire which had tumbled to an all time low like the German

Some of the crew at Bari harbour.

Chapter 12 - War's End

On the beach at Bari.

Myself on the beach at Bari with the boat we hired at a cost of 10 woodbines for the day, including the boatman!

Enjoying the very warm Adriatic waters.

Mark in the early 20s.

We caught the transport back to camp at 2300 and found our way to our billet. By now the temperature was more reasonable, in the 70s, so we all managed to get a good night's sleep. I awoke at 0700 to brilliant sunshine – it always did shine at this time of year. I noticed something outside of the window by my bed and putting out my hand I reached and picked several ripe figs – delicious! The whole of the domestic area must have been erected in an orchard; there were peach and fig trees everywhere. At breakfast we discovered that the standard of food was very good, and apart from the normal acceptable menu, at each meal there were innumerable bowls of fruit on the table; peaches and figs of course, plus a variety of melons, nectarines, etc. After five years of fruitless war time Britain, it was marvellous.

We were back in town the next day and again the afternoon was spent in swimming. The trip into town was very interesting. Along the coast ran the local tramway – a miniature steam engine with carriages. This ran right into Bari, the tracks running roughly parallel to the road. On the way into town we passed a cluster of gaily painted bungalows. On each side was the US Army sign "off limits". We learned that these were the local brothels. The first mile into town was very slummy, with tall gaunt houses on which no vestige of paint remained cheek by jowl with

Chapter 12 - War's End

Brothels on the outskirts of Bari. An American 'off limits' sign can be seen on the end house on the right of the photo.

tumbledown hovels – not at all interesting.

That night we missed the last transport back to camp, and because of our early take off we didn't dare risk staying at the Imperiale, so decided to walk back to camp hoping for a hitch on the way. We had been warned that walking back through the slums late at night was just not on. There had been many cases of Service personnel being attacked and robbed. As there were seven of us we were not too worried, in addition to which Harry and myself had tucked our .38s into our tunics. We started back for camp at midnight keeping to the centre of the road. There was a brilliant moon that helped a lot, but it was quite eerie to sense the local inhabitants hidden in the deep shadows of their doorsteps and alleyways with just an occasional glowing cigarette showing where they were. After walking three miles we flagged down an Army transport. The driver gladly gave us a lift back to the airfield. The following morning we picked up 20 excited looking soldiers for their long awaited leave. We set course for Tibbenham where we landed some eight hours later.

A week later we made our second trip to Bari. Upon our return there we discovered that there was a very good beach only a short walk from Camp. On this beach there was an excellent restaurant. It was run and managed by the Salvation Army for the benefit of all British and Allied personnel with food and drinks obtainable all day long and at very

View from a Birdcage

reasonable prices. It proved to be quite a haven for us, with good bathing right off the beach. This beach was all that could be wished for, and we spent the whole of our first day there alternately swimming and eating. Early that evening we decided to spend the night in Bari and sample the joys of the Imperiale. We booked in at 1800 and after a hurried meal walked down to the rather magnificent Opera House to see and hear an Italian opera performed - quite impressive.

On our second day there we decided to forego our customary swimming afternoon and explore the town during which I purchased two bottles of the local champagne for my friends the Bennetts back in Downham Market. I was also able to buy some nylons for Eileen, my current girl friend. Funny that these were unobtainable in England! This time we made sure of not missing the last bus back to Camp, and 24 hours later we were in the UK.

Our next trip in Italy, which was in fact our last, was again one week later. It followed the enjoyable pattern of our earlier trips and with the added bonus of an additional 48 hours stay, we were there four days in all. During the trip over one of the engines had been playing up - nothing too serious but causing us an hour's delay in our ETA. When the fault was reported to the Engineering Officer he said that repairs must be carried out before our return flight. The skills were available, but the spare part required was not so it had to be ordered from England and flown out to us on the next available flight. Thus we were able to enjoy an extension to our holiday. Strangely, when we eventually took off for home we were glad, for by now had had too much of the blazing sunshine and looked

On my way! Posted from Downham Market, September 1945. Taken at Bridge Farm.

184

Chapter 12 - War's End

forward to enjoying a cool English summer.

The day after our return, the chopper fell! We were all designated ex-aircrew and disbanded to await a posting to new non-flying duties. My first step was to an aircrew holding centre at Catterick in Yorkshire where I languished for seven days until I had my board. By now there was no way that an ex air gunner could get back on to flying, so I decided to keep as close to flying as was possible, and accepted a posting to Transport Command as a Passenger and Freight Officer. This involved assuming responsibilities for the safe loading of troop and freight aircraft and the disposal of inbound and outbound troops and cargo. Eventually I was posted to RAF Bramcote, near Nuneaton - an ex-Navy base. Here I did the course for my new job and, amongst other things, I was instructed into the mysteries of an aircraft load sheet and the centre of gravity of each type of aircraft on which I should be working. In the main, these would be Yorks, Lancasters and Liberators. Each of these aircraft had different centres of gravity. Providing that no diabolical errors were made in computing the load sheet, the only possible and embarrassing error that could be made was with the Liberator. This was a big aircraft with tricycle undercarriage, a long low fuselage and big twin fins and rudder. If, by error, one got the centre of gravity too far back, the aircraft would tilt back astern, leaving the nose wheel in the air and causing the tail end of the fuselage to drop down onto a metal skid. If this wasn't noticed at the time of take off (and apparently it wasn't noticed from the pilot's seat), the take off and landing was spectacular to say the least, with long streamers of vicious looking sparks issuing from where the metal skid was in contact with the runway. I only saw this happen once – fortunately not my responsibility.

When I had completed my training I was posted to RAF Bassingbourn in Transport Command. As a non-flyer (except from cadging passenger trips) I had a reasonably happy stay at this station. We worked shifts and I had one other officer, Flying Officer Bill Ford, to share the load. We had a reasonable number of staff working under us. One Warrant Officer, one Sergeant, two Corporals and a mixed bag of ten airmen and airwomen. Apart from the aforementioned duty of seeing to the safe loading of aircraft, we also had to attend to the needs of incoming troops, one of the benefits of this being that we had a 24 hour refreshment bar on the go. Our fairly large section and building also included HM Customs, though we had nothing to do with their work other than to advise them of the expected time of the arrival of incoming overseas flights.

View from a Birdcage

After being there a few months, I received my final posting which was to the Air Booking Centre in St James Street, London SW1. At this time, priorities were in force for any seats on passenger aircraft be they military or civilian. This had involved the setting up of a priorities board, comprising of Army, Royal Navy and Royal Air Force officers and their civilian counterparts. This board decided to order in priority of persons wishing to travel by air. All my work was of a clerical nature and my hours were civilian, 9 am to 6pm.

It was very comfortable being based in London because I had kept my flat on throughout the war. The work however was terribly boring. Only twice did I have something interesting to do, which on each occasion was to act as King's Messenger. One was a relatively straightforward run of the mill job, but the other gave me a nice weekend in Cornwall, my destination being RAF St Mawgan. This trip was in the middle of August, and upon arriving at Paddington I was overcome by a great feeling of guilt. There were long queues of holiday makers waiting to board the Atlantic Express. Being on state business I was escorted by the Stationmaster to a locked first class compartment. I was seen into the carriage, which was again locked with me inside. My instructions were to press the bell button if I wanted to go to the dining car or tend to the needs of nature, when the guard would let me out, which in due course he did. The same thing happened again when I made my one change at Par, although the remaining journey was quite short. I was met at Newquay station by an RAF saloon car and whisked away to the station where I handed over my case of documents. I had managed to get a 48 hour break whilst I was there, so was able to sample the joys of surf riding at Newquay.

My return journey was interesting. Although I was travelling first class, I had no diplomatic bag, so there was no locking me up on my own. At Par I managed to get a seat, but shortly afterwards noticed that in the crowded corridor adjacent to my carriage, a middle aged lady was standing. She graciously accepted the offer of my seat, and when I stood outside, a gentleman who had been accompanying her said to me "The lady to whom you gave your seat was the well known authoress Daphne du Maurier". Since I had always enjoyed her books I was pleased to have been of service.

At the final stage in my RAF career, which was fast coming to an end, I was sorely tempted to apply for a permanent commission. My boss, a Wing Commander, was on the board to which I would have to apply, and

Chapter 12 - War's End

he was of the opinion that I would pass and obtain a P/C without too much difficulty, though with the lower rank of Pilot Officer. I was very tempted for I was fond of service life, even though grounded.

Eventually, after much heart searching, I decided not to apply. My reasons were two-fold, one being that I had just become engaged to be married. I realised that since all of my war service had been in the UK, upon receipt of a permanent commission this was certain to be followed by an overseas posting. From a personal choice I would have enjoyed this immensely, and I could certainly have taken my wife to France, Germany, Italy or anywhere in Europe. However the likelihood was that I should be posted to somewhere like Okinawa in the Pacific or to Sharjah in the Persian Gulf. Neither area was considered suitable for white women. The other reason was my employers, and it weighed heavily on my conscience. For seven years, both the time that I was in the fire service and in the RAF, they had been making up my salary, and I just couldn't see myself disregarding their generosity and calmly saying "Goodbye"!

After a further six months service at the Air Booking Office, I became a civilian once again.

APPENDIX

1 The nautical term of port and starboard for left and right were used exclusively as far as aircraft and flying were concerned, and were taken in the direction in which the aircraft was travelling, either on the ground or in the air. Port side of the aircraft was always on or to the left, starboard on or towards the right. During my initial training I, and most gunners, had considerable difficulty in getting this weighed up because a rear gunner sits with his back to the direction in which the aircraft is flying, thus at first the obvious tendency was for the gunner to call his right hand starboard and his left hand port. In other words, the reverse to what was actually correct. In due course I eventually got this sorted out, but not without a lot of worry over a period of several weeks. Strangely enough I never heard of a mid-upper gunner having the same problem, although theoretically it should have been worse for them because they could face fore or aft! The other nautical term in use by the Royal Air Force was the nautical mile in which distances were calculated.

2 If night vision was lost due to sudden unexpected exposure to light, then for some 15-20 minutes the gunner would be technically blind insofar as perfect night vision was concerned. Night vision had been the subject of a very careful study by the Royal Air Force, and air gunners in particular were expected to put in some very regular training on this subject. We worked hard in our section each week having a variety of exercises and tests. Without going too deeply into the technicalities of night blindness, this very briefly is what it is about. When going out into the dark after leaving very bright lights, it takes the average person's eyes approximately 15-20 minutes to become acclimatised and night sight adapted – that is 100% adapted. During the war, under blackout conditions, all of us had the experience of going out of doors into the darkness and for a while stumbling around and bumping into obstructions until becoming acclimatised to the darkness. Gradually, obstructions begin to show up more clearly. On operations, the danger is that having

Appendix

been caught in a searchlight or in the light given off by an explosion, the night vision is damaged temporarily, so that an enemy fighter pilot who has not suffered from the same disability would be enabled to come in at close quarters, getting a burst into the bomber before the gunners were able to see their attacker. To minimise the danger, whenever it was possible to foresee the likelihood of conditions of unexpected brilliance, the gunner closed one eye thereby retaining the good night vision in one eye while continuing the search with the other eye. In this way, should the aircraft be coned in searchlights, then as soon as it was free of lights, the gunner opened the eye that had been closed. This method of retaining some night vision had some merit and seemed to work.

3 Our recent coning in the searchlights had brought back to mind what was probably our worst experience of this particular hazard. Some months before, we had been briefed for an attack on Nantes on the Atlantic coast of France. The target was an important marshalling yard on the railway through which went vast quantities of war supplies for the submarine bases and pens at St Nazaire. The briefing was quite straightforward and little trouble was anticipated. Only the Met forecast was problematical, which on this occasion was very uncertain. It was believed that when we reached the target there would be good visibility below from our normal bombing height of 18-20,000 feet. However, in the event of cloud cover the importance of pin pointing the target required that we should make every effort to bomb visually and not rely on H_2S or sky markers. In other words, go down below the cloud base if necessary.

We went off happily, convinced that the trip would be a doddle. The outbound journey passed almost without incident, other than a minor alarm when we were over the Channel Islands. "Fishpond", our downward looking radar, was operating and Nobby had seen what appeared to be German night fighters on the screen. These would probably be from the German airfield on Jersey. We were flying in the clear, though there was cloud cover below us. A very sharp look out was kept by us all, but fortunately no attacks developed and eventually all became quiet once again.

During the remainder of the trip to the target, cloud built up to our level, and by the time that we had reached the target area it was 10/10ths. With nil visibility below, Emmie decided that we should go down below the cloud base, so down we went, 15,000 feet, 12,000 feet, 8,000 feet, and 4,000 feet and still in cloud. At 3,000 feet we came out below the cloud base, and what a sight! Right in the target area there were searchlights and flak everywhere. All the flak was predicted, and on our bombing run they gave us hell. Because of our low level the medium flak guns, which did not normally bother us, were on this occasion able to reach us without any trouble, and although we suffered no direct hits, we were constantly aware that shell fragments were hitting the fuselage. After a frightening lapse of time our bombs had been dropped, the photo had been taken, and up we climbed for the comparative safety of the clouds.

Immediately that we commenced the climb we were coned by searchlights and every gun seemed to turn in our direction. There were still no direct hits but the near misses were frightening. Afterwards I swore that we were so low that the German soldiers were firing at us with their rifles. As our climb steepened, both Red and I fired continuously down the searchlight beams, long burst that use up a lot of ammunition. Almost at once a searchlight beam went out. This cheered us up immensely. We both thought that there was a very good possibility that we had hit the searchlight or its crew.

We bore on through the clouds, and after a while broke through the tops at 21,000 feet into beautiful moonlight. By now my nerves had quietened down and I had resumed my search when another Lancaster broke cloud cover a few hundred yards away from us. For a moment I watched him, then noticed twinkling lights from the centre and end of the aircraft. Suddenly the penny dropped! I pressed the intercom button and shouted, "Rear gunner to Pilot, dive port – we are being fired on by another Lancaster". We went immediately into a very steep dive into the cloud below, where we stayed for 15 minutes, then gingerly climbed back above the cloud tops. With all of the crew very much on the lookout, we were able to see that the sky was deserted and we bore steadily on towards the English coast.

I pondered over the foolishness of the two gunners on the other Lanc. No doubt they too had had a frightening time over the target, and were understandably twitchy when breaking cloud cover. However there really was no excuse for firing at us in view of the remarkably good light conditions above the clouds. There had been many occasions in the past when I had held my fire because of some doubt when seeing a very dim shape and this had been when we were in thin cloud. I always watched for the number of exhausts glowing, or some near positive proof of identity before opening fire.

The end of the story is yet to come! An hour or so later we were in

Appendix

the circuit at Downham Market and on our final approach for landing. As soon as we touched down, we veered to port and onto the grass. Emmie was eventually able to pull us up when we were quite close to the control tower. We all quickly clambered out, in case of fire and walked round to the front of Willie, where the cause of our dicey landing was immediately apparent – our port tyre was punctured. We all praised Emmie on his usual display of aplomb when faced with the need for immediate and vital action.

The following morning we all went along to the maintenance hangar. The cause of the trouble was quickly confirmed. One of the gunners of the Lanc that had fired on us the previous evening had hit the undercarriage cowling and the bullet had penetrated the port tyre. The proof lay on the Flight Sergeant's table – a British .303 bullet. So much for what we thought was to be an easy trip!

4 During one such blitz on London, while I was still in the Fire service, my household been hit by an incendiary bomb. Fortunately it had caught the edge of the gutter and had fallen into the garden on its side without exploding. For a year or two it stood in place of honour, on my mantelpiece, still fully alive (a fall from three feet was very unlikely to have caused it to explode!) A few years later when I was on leave from the RAF, I thought of the incendiary, and took it back with me to Camp. A few days later we were briefed for a raid on Lubeck, and I chalked on the side of the incendiary a very rude and pertinent message. I took it with me in my turret and eventually threw it out onto the blazing target below, hopefully with better effect than on the previous occasion that it had been dropped.

5 When caught in predicted flak every effort must be made to confuse the gun crews operating the predictor by diving, climbing and weaving, a combination of all three. If caught in a box barrage however, this would have been a futile exercise. In such a barrage a very large concentration of guns were set to fire in an imaginary box in the sky. This box could be, perhaps, two miles square and half a mile deep. It was therefore impossible to confuse the gunners and predictors, and the drill was to fly straight and level through it, maintaining the highest possible speed, thus lessening the time spent in this hazardous area. Under these circumstances one's chances were in the hands of God.

On an earlier trip we had experienced a frightening box barrage. The

View from a Birdcage

raid took place in daylight on a brilliantly sunny day. The target was Trossy St Maximin, fairly close to Paris. We had successfully bombed and were on our way home, about midway between Paris and the coast, when we ran into this particularly vicious box. We were in company with another 635 Squadron aircraft and were both boring through the barrage. Suddenly we experienced a very near hit and the fuselage was splattered with shell fragments. As usual on such occasions, Emmie called each of us up in turn to make sure that no one had been hurt. We all replied except Red. After further unsuccessful attempts to contact him without any response, Frank and Nobby went back to the mid upper turret and found him unconscious, slumped in his seat. They managed to get him out and on to the rest bed. There were no apparent injuries and after a few seconds he recovered consciousness. In fact, it turned out that the burst had been so close that he had been rendered unconscious by the blast of the shell. This was borne out by the fact that the turret Perspex had been shattered.

In this same barrage one other aircraft was badly hit and caught fire. We saw it going down and some of the crew bailing out. It was captained by Sqn Ldr Ian Bazalgette, a splendid and experienced pilot, but skill alone could not get you out of a haphazard box barrage. The pilot stayed with his aircraft enabling those of his crew who could do so to bale out. He then tried without success to land the crippled aircraft and save the lives of his injured crew members. Sadly, he and the remainder of his crew were killed. For this gallant act he received the posthumous award of the Victoria Cross. He was sadly missed by us all on 635.

6 With regard to air combats generally. When we first arrived on the Squadron, the Gunnery leader gave us and the other new crews his customary welcome lecture. During the talk that followed, we were very surprised when he said "If I find any of you gunners reporting combats on all of your operations, you'll be out of the Pathfinder Force without delay because you'll not be the types that we want!" Seeing our natural astonishment he then went on to explain, that unlike fighter pilots, our job was to get to the target and bomb, returning with the crew intact. Combats of course could not be avoided forever, but if the gunners were doing their jobs properly by maintaining a vigilant and ceaseless search, most attacks could be forestalled, or minimised, by the gunners giving the pilot early evasive action. Our chief job was to help in the successful hitting of the target, not to pile up massive scores imaginary or otherwise!

Appendix

Over the months that followed we all saw how true this was. Although the occasional combats were unavoidable, by the early sighting of enemy fighters we had been able to avoid far more combats than those that we had actually been engaged in. Since that lecture, we knew of one of the station crews whose gunners had been posted away for this reason.

7   The refreshment bar at Bassingbourn proved to be my undoing! One day I became aware that my mouth felt most uncomfortable, noticing that my gums were puffy and swollen. I put up with it for two days, by which time I was getting no sleep at night. In desperation I reported to the Dental Section at SSQ and upon being examined, was told that I had "Vincents" (trench mouth). This had been rampant at that time amongst the troops in India from where most of my incoming passengers arrived. It seemed that I had caught the trench mouth as a result of drinking from a cup that had not been washed properly in our own Section kitchen.

The treatment, which lasted for some days, consisted of intense mouth irrigation of almost neat "Milton". At the end of this treatment I was free of infection - but the inside of my mouth was like a prune, due to the astringent properties of Milton. As a final addition to my miseries, the dental officer told me that I had two impacted wisdom teeth. Arrangements were then made for me to go to the RAF Hospital at Ely. I went there for a week during which time the offending molars were chiselled out!